THE EVERYTHING

GREEN SMOOTHIES BOOK

Dear Reader,

Every day, we seem to have a million things to do; between our hectic jobs, family schedules, household chores, errands, shopping, and the unexpected to-do's that pop up throughout the day, our nutrition seems to be one area that doesn't get the attention it deserves. In writing this book, my goal was to make the need for green smoothies obvious while showing how simple it can be to implement them into your daily life. As a personal trainer and mother of two small children, I have seen the amazing improvements in every aspect of my life, and theirs, from indulging in just one green smoothie a day. That's right: Not only can you create delicious smoothies that you will wholeheartedly enjoy, but kids love them, too.

No matter what it is you're looking for, you can probably find it at the bottom of a green smoothie glass. Want more energy and stamina, better focus, more efficient fat loss, healthier digestion, less illness, beautiful skin and hair, or to look and feel younger? All of these things can be achieved and improved with green smoothies. So, congratulations for taking this step to amazing health and wellness, and enjoy!

Britt Brandon

Welcome to the EVERYTHING® Series!

These handy, accessible books give you all you need to tackle a difficult project, gain a new hobby, comprehend a fascinating topic, prepare for an exam, or even brush up on something you learned back in school but have since forgotten.

You can choose to read an *Everything*® book from cover to cover or just pick out the information you want from our four useful boxes: e-questions, e-facts, e-alerts, and e-ssentials.

We give you everything you need to know on the subject, but throw in a lot of fun stuff along the way, too.

We now have more than 400 *Everything*® books in print, spanning such wide-ranging categories as weddings, pregnancy, cooking, music instruction, foreign language, crafts, pets, New Age, and so much more. When you're done reading them all, you can finally say you know *Everything*®!

QUESTION

Answers to common questions

FACT

Important snippets of information

ALERT

Urgent warnings

ESSENTIAL

Quick handy tips

PUBLISHER Karen Cooper

DIRECTOR OF ACQUISITIONS AND INNOVATION Paula Munier

MANAGING EDITOR, EVERYTHING® SERIES Lisa Laing

COPY CHIEF Casey Ebert

ASSISTANT PRODUCTION EDITOR Jacob Erickson

ACQUISITIONS EDITOR Hillary Thompson

ASSOCIATE DEVELOPMENT EDITOR Hillary Thompson

EDITORIAL ASSISTANT Ross Weisman

EVERYTHING® SERIES COVER DESIGNER Erin Alexander

LAYOUT DESIGNERS Colleen Cunningham, Elisabeth Lariviere, Ashley Vierra, Denise Wallace

Visit the entire Everything® series at *www.everything.com*

THE EVERYTHING®

GREEN SMOOTHIES BOOK

Britt Brandon with Lorena Novak Bull, RD

Adamsmedia

Avon, Massachusetts

To my amazing daughters, Lilly and Lonni,
for inspiring me every day! To my wonderful husband,
Jimmy, for all of your love and support.

An Everything® Series Book.
Everything® and everything.com® are registered trademarks of F+W Media, Inc.

Contains material adapted and abridged from *The Everything® Juicing Book* by Carole Jacobs, Chef
Patrice Johnson, and Nicole Cormier, RD, copyright © 2010 by F+W Media, Inc., ISBN 10: 1-4405-0326-5,
ISBN 13: 978-1-4405-0326-9.

Published by Adams Media, a division of F+W Media, Inc.
57 Littlefield Street, Avon, MA 02322 U.S.A.
www.adamsmedia.com

ISBN 10: 1-4405-2564-1
ISBN 13: 978-1-4405-2564-3
eISBN 10: 1-4405-2595-1
eISBN 13: 978-1-4405-2595-7

Printed in the United States of America.

10 9 8 7 6 5

Library of Congress Cataloging-in-Publication Data
is available from the publisher.

This publication is designed to provide accurate and authoritative information with regard to the subject matter covered. It is sold with the understanding that the publisher is not engaged in rendering legal,
accounting, or other professional advice. If legal advice or other expert assistance is required, the services
of a competent professional person should be sought.

—From a *Declaration of Principles* jointly adopted by a Committee of the
American Bar Association and a Committee of Publishers and Associations

Many of the designations used by manufacturers and sellers to distinguish their products are claimed as
trademarks. Where those designations appear in this book and Adams Media was aware of a trademark
claim, the designations have been printed with initial capital letters.

The information in this book should not be used for diagnosing or treating any health problem. Not all diet
and exercise plans suit everyone. You should always consult a trained medical professional before starting
a diet, taking any form of medication, or embarking on any fitness or weight-training program. The author
and publisher disclaim any liability arising directly or indirectly from the use of this book.

This book is available at quantity discounts for bulk purchases.
For information, please call 1-800-289-0963.

Contents

Introduction

WITH ALL OF THE research that shows how important it is to consume vegetables and fruit, how is it that the Standard American Diet (SAD) is so lacking in these two food groups? To some, daily meals consist of unhealthy takeout, fast food, fried foods, or just plain unbalanced nutrition. All of the reasons for eating these simple, fast, or "inexpensive" foods that don't provide the nourishment your body needs are well founded: There's not enough time to prepare healthy meals, not enough money to purchase them consistently, or too many schedule conflicts to eat proper meals when your body needs them. As a result of consuming these less-than-nutritious foods, the average person is left wanting more energy and stamina, struggles with weight loss, and desires clearer skin, better digestion, less illness, and the vibrant feeling of overall health. How can you improve your diet? How can you improve your quality of life?

The answer to all of these issues can be found right here in this book. Green smoothies take just minutes to prepare, serve, and consume. Spending less than you'd expect (and saving on doctor's visits and medications), you'll be pleasantly surprised to see how easily green smoothies can become part of your daily routine. In addition to the low cost, you'll have peace of mind knowing exactly what you're consuming, where it came from, and how it was prepared. You'll recognize the benefits of green smoothies in just a matter of days or weeks, and see for yourself the power of the green smoothie. You'll never go back to life without them!

With Dr. Oz's powerful endorsement on the *Oprah* show on New Year's Day 2006, green smoothies got a sudden spotlight and the attention of millions of television viewers around the world. Although information about the benefits of leafy greens and other vibrant fruits and vegetables has always been available, the idea of a "green" smoothie may not have appealed to the average consumer. With the outstanding nutrition, proven health benefits, and newfound health and vivacity provided by these simple drinks that take such little time to make, why would you not be interested, intrigued, or just curious enough to give them a try? If you want more for your body, mind, and future, the results are clear: Green smoothies can (and will) change your life!

CHAPTER 1

Green Smoothie Basics

Although the value of a diet rich in greens, fruits, and vegetables has been well known for quite some time, the green smoothie has not been commonplace until recent years. It has also been only in recent years that much of the information has been provided identifying the Standard American Diet as the main culprit in multiple health issues that strike people of all ages and backgrounds. With the breakthrough of raw-food diets, the proven health benefits of diets low in refined carbohydrates, and illnesses that have shown marked improvement with the implementation of a more green-focused diet, green smoothies now appeal to more people.

What Are Green Smoothies?

A green smoothie is a mixture of greens and fruit blended together until a desirable, smooth texture is achieved. While there are many smoothie combinations that target specific needs or areas of the body, the main reasons to consume green smoothies are to eat more vegetables and fruits on a daily basis, enjoy the green smoothie combinations you choose from this book and create on your own, and live a healthier and happier lifestyle as a result of this major nutritional shift in your daily life. Integrating these smoothies into your average day without extra time, money, or hassle is also easily done. It takes only minutes to prepare, blend, and enjoy these green treats, and requires only a blender and the vegetables and fruits of your choosing. The entire process is easy to understand and apply to any schedule—no matter how hectic.

From children to adults, and pregnant women to raw-food enthusiasts, everyone is including green smoothies in their diets. Those who desire a faster metabolism and those who suffer from serious ailments can all find benefits from green smoothies and the powerful ingredients packed in each sip. Combinations can be mixed, matched, and manipulated to create any type of green smoothie desired. Bright morning smoothies and sweet dessert smoothies are filled with important nutrition and tasty additions while savory smoothies can be made from a number of ingredients to satisfy any salty or spicy craving.

Greens and Nutrition

Green smoothies are smoothies with greens blended into them. They differ from juices in that they're a complete food—they still have fiber. Most people know that greens are very nutritious, but struggle to eat enough of them—they're not the easiest vegetables to prepare tastefully while maintaining all of the important vitamins and minerals your body requires. Steaming, sautéing, baking, and roasting vegetables causes them to lose the vitamins and minerals you're trying to consume by eating them in the first place. Greens can also be hard to digest—you may not get the full benefits from your average meal or salad containing greens because the greens themselves can be difficult to digest and tedious to chew to the point where digestion would be easy. Blended greens in smoothies have already been ripped apart and are effectively "predigested," allowing for almost immediate absorption.

FACT

The blending process used in green smoothies actually breaks down the cellulose in the greens, making the nutrients able to be absorbed 70 percent to 90 percent more than that of a traditional salad.

Although many suffer from irregularity, few know of the power of fiber held in a serving of greens. A type of carbohydrate that resists the body's digestive enzymes and acids, soluble fiber forms a gel-like substance in the digestive tract that binds with cholesterol so it can't be reabsorbed by the body. Insoluble fiber (often referred to as "nature's broom") moves food through the digestive system more quickly, reducing instances of constipation. Increasing your daily intake of deep-green vegetables and certain fruits can make irregularity a thing of the past.

Green Smoothies Versus the Standard American Diet

When you take into consideration that the Standard American Diet is packed with high levels of sugars, sodium, saturated fats, and preservatives from the types of foods consumed and how those foods are prepared, the green smoothie can be a very important addition to any diet. Regular consumption of empty calories and dangerous additives can easily be changed, and consuming these nutrient-dense smoothies just once a day can reverse the adverse affects of such nutrient-deficient lifestyles. Between a skipped breakfast, a lunch on the run from a fast-food place, and a dinner made from ingredients packed with sodium, trans fats, and dangerous preservatives, the average consumer rarely fulfills the suggested serving sizes of fruits and vegetables in a normal day and ends up suffering from the symptoms and illnesses that result from important deficiencies. All of these ailments can be reversed and improved with green smoothies and their powerful ingredients.

Supplement Your Diet Naturally

Symptoms and illnesses that arise from a vitamin deficiency can only be cured by that particular vitamin, which makes deep-green vegetables a one-stop shop for ensuring you fulfill your body's needs for vitamins and negate any possible illnesses and symptoms that could arise from being deficient. Also, of the eight essential amino acids that we need for bodily functions such as muscle repair, manufacturing hormones, mental functions, sleep, memory, and physical and mental energy, your body does not produce any naturally, so you need to get them from the foods you consume.

QUESTION

What are some of the benefits I'll receive from drinking green smoothies?
The vegetables, fruits, and herbs used in your green smoothies are rich in powerful antioxidants known for enhancing brain function, combating negative effects of stress, improving cardiovascular health, and reversing the aging process.

How many essential amino acids do you think are in a processed and unidentifiable fast-food hamburger? Whatever the answer may be, it can't compare to the raw vegetables and raw fruits you'll be blending into your green smoothie. If you know you are lacking in a vitamins, minerals, or amino acids, green smoothies are a great way to meet and exceed your dietary needs.

Of all of the vitamins and minerals absolutely required by the body, each green smoothie ingredient packs a powerful amount in order to keep your body and mind working at its fullest potential.

Vitamins

- **Biotin.** Found in the deep-green leafy vegetables, biotin is responsible for cell growth, maintaining a steady blood sugar level, and the metabolism of fats and amino acids. It also strengthens hair and nails.
- **Carotenes.** Vibrant orange and yellow vegetables and leafy greens get their color from this amazing vitamin that is a powerful antioxidant. It provides protection from free radicals and aids in cancer prevention. Important phytochemicals lutein, lycopene, and beta-carotene are released with the tearing of these vegetables and provide the body with enormous protection from illness and disease.
- **Vitamin A.** Carrots and dark-green and yellow vegetables hold this important vitamin known for its role in providing vision health and proper cell growth.
- **Vitamin B1.** Also known as thiamin, B1 aids in every process, including nervous system processes, muscle function, metabolism of carbohydrates, and the production of healthy digestive enzymes as well as electrolyte flow. This vitamin can be found in oranges and certain citrus fruits.
- **Vitamin B12.** Also known as cobalamin, this vitamin aids in blood formation, energy production, and is necessary for the metabolism of every cell throughout the body.
- **Vitamin B2.** Also known as riboflavin, this vitamin found mainly in broccoli and asparagus aids cells in their growth, maintains proper functioning, and produces energy.

- **Vitamin B3.** Also known as niacin, this hormone-regulating vitamin assists the adrenal glands in production of sex- and stress-related hormones, lowers LDL ("bad" cholesterol) while raising HDL ("good" cholesterol), and has been recently suggested to improve symptoms of arthritis.
- **Vitamin B5.** Also known as pantothenic acid, this vitamin is responsible for synthesizing and metabolizing the fats, carbohydrates, and proteins for all necessary bodily functions.
- **Vitamin B6.** Also known as pyridoxine, B6 is found in peas, carrots, and spinach and is responsible for the synthesis of important neurotransmitters serotonin and norepinephrine.
- **Vitamin C.** Found in most citrus fruits and in vibrant-colored and deep-green vegetables, vitamin C is well known for its immune-boosting properties but is also necessary for iron absorption and supports the growth and repair of cartilage, collagen, muscle, and blood vessels.
- **Vitamin D.** Produced in our bodies as a result of exposure to the sun, you need helpful supplies of vitamin D from plant sources in order to protect your body from autoimmune diseases, cancers, osteoporosis, and hypertension.
- **Vitamin E.** This fat-soluble antioxidant has been known for stimulating skin repair and strengthening cells, but it is absolutely necessary in removing free radicals from the body's systems. It is found in abundance in spinach, collards, and dandelion greens, as well as turnips and beets.
- **Vitamin K.** This fat-soluble compound is extremely helpful in blood clotting and is found in the deep-green leafy vegetables.

Minerals

- **Boron.** Found in spinach, cabbage, and carrots, as well as apples, pears, and grapes, this mineral maintains the health of bones and teeth by metabolizing calcium, magnesium, and phosphorous. It has also been cited for building muscle and promoting mental clarity and brain functioning.
- **Calcium.** Although well known for maintaining the strength of bones and teeth, calcium also plays a vital role in maintaining regularity of

the heart and helping to metabolize iron efficiently. Found in kale, broccoli, and collard greens, calcium is especially important for women who are pregnant, nursing, or menstruating.

- **Chromium.** This weight-loss helper is powerful in effective fatty-acid metabolism and works together with insulin to maintain the proper use of sugar in the body.
- **Copper.** Found in most green vegetables, copper is another mineral that aids in the absorption of iron, but also helps to maintain cardiovascular health and can promote fertility in both men and women.
- **Selenium.** Found in deep-green vegetables (notably asparagus) and mushrooms, selenium is helpful in weight loss by stimulating the metabolism, and effective in disease prevention by acting as an antioxidant against free radicals that cause health issues like arthritis, cancer, and heart disease.
- **Magnesium.** Helpful in maintaining proper functioning of the muscles and the nervous system. Health problems resulting from low levels of magnesium include hypertension, diabetes, osteoporosis, and certain digestive disorders.
- **Potassium.** Working with sodium to maintain a proper balance of the body's water, potassium is mainly required for the metabolism of carbohydrates and the synthesis of proteins.
- **Sodium.** This mineral is important in maintaining proper muscle control and optimal nerve functioning, as well as correcting the body's distribution of fluid and maintaining proper pH balance.
- **Iron.** Although all people require adequate amounts of iron found in dark-green vegetables, vegans and pregnant or menstruating women are in a different bracket, requiring much more. The reason iron is such a commodity for lifestyles requiring additional protein is that it is mainly responsible for strengthening the immune system, and it is found in great amounts in the proteins of red blood cells.

Greens and Healing

With many new diagnoses, doctors' orders normally include a change of diet, and that changed diet usually includes an increase of fruits and vegetables while decreasing refined carbohydrate and sugar intake. The studies, statistics, and testimonies of those that have introduced greens into their diet speak loudly in terms of the resulting physical and mental health improvements. Researchers at Harvard Medical School tracked the health of more than 22,000 physicians and found that those who ate at least 2½ servings of vegetables daily reduced their risk of heart disease by almost 25 percent. At the University of California, Berkeley, researchers found that a high intake of fruits and vegetables also reduced the risk of cancer on an average of 50 percent. And a vegan diet rich in fruits and vegetables has reportedly reduced diabetes indicators and shown an increase in immune protection against arthritis.

FACT

Many people who add green smoothies to their diet experience the benefits within a matter of days or few short weeks. These benefits include more energy, mental clarity, better digestion, and clearer skin.

Women and men have found their hair feels stronger, thicker, and more lustrous as a result of taking important vitamins like calcium, magnesium, and biotin that are found in greens. Men and women have reported a sense of mental clarity that can be compared to "the clearing of a fog" when they started consuming green smoothies; almost every mineral, vitamin, and phytonutrient found in deep greens can aid in mental and physical processes.

Reduce Your Health Risks

From improving the condition of hair, skin, and nails to a renewed mental clarity and increased stamina, green smoothies combine the perfect ingredients to provide the essential vitamins, minerals, and nutrients to achieve almost any change desired. Vitamins necessary to sustain life and maintain healthy lifestyles can be found in deep greens and fruits. Folate (folic acid), found in many of the greens, is an important B-vitamin needed especially by pregnant women in order to ensure the fetus is protected from spinal defects like spina bifida. The protein provided by vegetable sources far surpasses that of meats of any variety; a deep-green vegetable like broccoli can deliver a healthy dose of protein without the unhealthy saturated fats of an animal protein source.

ALERT

Vegetable juices and tonics found in the common marketplace can be packed with sodium and preservatives. By creating your own green smoothie, you know and control exactly what goes into every sip.

The powerful ingredients found in green smoothies have alleviated conditions even as severe as osteoarthritis, osteoporosis, Alzheimer's, and various cancers. The phytochemicals found in these greens have been proven to have antioxidant activity that protects cells from oxidative damage and reduces the risks for certain cancers. If you like cabbage, you'll be pleased to learn that it contains indoles that stimulate enzymes that make estrogen less effective, and can reduce the risk of breast cancer!

Preparation and Storage Tips

In order to prepare a green smoothie, all that's needed are the fruits and vegetables of your choosing (according to recipes that sound appetizing to you) and a high-speed blender capable of emulsifying the greens and additions. The blender needed for green smoothies can be completely based on your needs and choosing. In most reviews of blenders on the market today, green smoothie consumers compare them based upon a couple of major factors: power, noise, capacity, and ease of cleanup.

- **Power.** The power of your blender will determine how quickly and efficiently your smoothie and its ingredients can be liquefied and blended. If time or texture are of no importance, this factor may not require much attention.
- **Noise.** Noise can be of no importance or of the utmost importance when it comes to selecting the perfect blender. If you plan on blending your smoothie prior to the rest of your house waking, it might be smart to invest in a quieter version that will still get the job done nicely.

- **Capacity.** Capacity is extremely important, considering you will be putting cups of fruits and vegetables, along with other ingredients, into the same canister. You will need enough room for the blending to be efficient. Also, be sure to take into consideration that you will need enough room in your blender for the adequate amount of ingredients for your desired number of servings.
- **Ease of cleanup.** Although cleanup may also seem like a nonissue at first thought, consider your schedule or routine when making this purchase. Do you need it to be dishwasher safe? Will the blender require special tools for cleaning? Is there a recommended strategy to keep the blender clean while also ensuring a long lifespan?

The two most commonly used brands are Blendtec and Vitamix. Although these high-speed emulsifying machines come at a higher cost than your average blender, the quality, efficiency, and capabilities can make even those reluctant to purchase a new one consider making a swap. If you plan to use blenders for this precise purpose, more familiar brand names like KitchenAid, Black and Decker, and Krups also provide smoothie makers or blenders that will leave you delighted.

ESSENTIAL

Creating a green smoothie with organic fruits and vegetables ensures your tasty treat is free of dyes, pesticides, and preservatives.

Shelf Life

The prep time required for the ingredients starts as soon as you get your greens, fruits, and vegetables home. Although greens will remain green for days or weeks, their powerful antioxidants, vitamins, and minerals dissipate from the time of picking, so eating them as soon as possible ensures you are getting the most nutrition out of every ounce. It has been determined that lettuces and greens should be washed and stored in an airtight bag or container with paper towels or something that can claim excess water on the leaves. Some vegetables such as carrots, turnips, and beets should be rid of their stems and green tops in order to prevent drying the vegetables out. Both fruits and vegetables with hard outer skins or rinds should be peeled prior to blending, and pits should always be removed. After blending your green smoothie, you can even take it to go in any insulated container that will help maintain its temperature and freshness, or you can store it in an airtight glass container in your refrigerator for up to three days (although it probably won't last that long!).

Pantry Essentials

The simplicity of green smoothies is found in what is required to create one: a blender, a knife for food prep, and the greens, fruits, and vegetables of your choosing. That's it! Whether you'd like to use your tried-and-true kitchen blender or you'd rather opt for a high-horsepower emulsifying machine, the choice is yours. A cutting board, peeler, and knife will help in cleaning and preparing your fruits and vegetables with ease and assist in quick clean up. In most cases, you may want to soak and rinse your greens in cold water, but rinsing by hand can be done just as easily. Salad spinners offer the option of spinning off any excess water from your greens.

FACT

In a fraction of the time required to make an entire meal, you can prep, blend, and enjoy a more nutritious green smoothie. Green smoothies can also cut down on the cost of preparing an entire meal.

Depending upon the type, taste, or texture you desire, your ingredients will be the main priority throughout the smoothie-making process. The choice of greens, vegetables, and fruits that you'd like to combine in your smoothie are essential, and you can always stock up on any of the suggested additions you find appealing. Although certain fruits and vegetables may not be available locally or seasonally depending upon the time of year, freezing is always an option that will allow you to enjoy your favorite ingredients year round.

Additional Ingredients

Soy and protein powders, Spirulina, coconut milk, almond milk, rice milk, kefir, Greek-style yogurt, and cacao are tasty ingredients you can blend into your own green smoothies. These ingredients are widely available and can change the taste experience completely. The bottom line is that what you need in your pantry is what *you* would like in your green smoothie. Try one ingredient, or try them all—it's up to you!

CHAPTER 2

Key Ingredients

Deep-green, organic produce is the best choice for your green smoothies. If you're concerned about the "pricey" costs of organic produce from your local market, considering growing fruits and vegetables in your backyard garden is the easiest way to save money while also ensuring your ingredients haven't been contaminated by dangerous herbicides or pesticides. Organic produce doesn't expose you to the dangerous chemicals used in commercial agriculture, ensuring that you'll get maximum nutrients from the fruits and vegetables you use. If you don't have the time or space to grow your own, purchase locally or regionally grown organic produce in your local health food store, farmer's market, or supermarket.

Leafy Greens

Your green smoothie isn't complete without a dose of vibrant leafy greens. Research shows that leafy greens are one of the most concentrated sources of nutrition. They supply iron, calcium, potassium, magnesium, vitamins K, C, E, B6, and B12, and folate in abundance.

Leafy greens provide a variety of phytonutrients, including beta-carotene and lutein, which protect cells from damage and eyes from age-related problems. A few cups of dark green leaves also contain small amounts of omega-3 fatty acids and nine times the RDA for vitamin K, which regulates blood clotting, protects bones from osteoporosis, and may reduce the risk of atherosclerosis by reducing calcium in arterial plaques.

A Dieter's Delight

Because greens have very few carbohydrates and a lot of fiber, they take the body a long time to digest. If you're on a diet, leafy greens can be your best friend; they fill you up, but they have very few calories and no fat. In fact, most greens have such little impact on blood glucose that many low-carb diets consider them free foods.

Types of Greens

Leafy greens run the gamut in taste, from arugula—which ancient Romans considered an aphrodisiac because of its peppery taste—to iceberg lettuce, which is crunchy and sweet with a very mild flavor. Here are some of the most popular leafy greens used for smoothies:

- **Lettuce.** Deep-green lettuce is a good source of calcium, chlorophyll, iron, magnesium, potassium, silicon, and vitamins A and E. All types help rebuild hemoglobin, add shine and thickness to hair, and promote hair growth. Iceberg contains natural opiates that relax the muscles and nerves. Lettuce is strong and works best in combination with other vegetables. Wash carefully, refrigerate, and use within a few days.
- **Frisée and escarole.** Both from the endive family, frisée is the curly leafed, light-green variety with a mild flavor, while escarole is a more broad-leafed deep green that can be bitter if not selected carefully.

Both varieties are high in vitamins A and K, folate, and beta-carotene and are known for fighting depression and calming food cravings.

- **Parsley.** Packed with chlorophyll, vitamins A and C, calcium, magnesium, phosphorous, potassium, sodium, and sulfur, parsley helps stimulate oxygen metabolism, cell respiration, and regeneration. Wash, refrigerate, and use within five days.

- **Spinach, kale, and Swiss chard.** Popeye was right all along: You'll be strong to the finish if you eat your spinach, kale, and chard, which are similar in nutritional value and provide ample supplies of iron, phosphorous, fiber, and vitamins A, B, C, E, and K. Wash thoroughly and bag loosely in the refrigerator. Use within four days.

- **Watercress.** This delicate, leafy green veggie has a slightly pungent taste and is packed with vitamin C, calcium, and potassium. It also contains acid-forming minerals, which make it ideal for intestinal cleansing and normalizing, and chlorophyll, which stimulates metabolism and circulatory functions. Refrigerate and use within five days.

- **Wheatgrass.** The juice from wheat berries contains many antiaging properties, including vitamins A, B complex, and E, chlorophyll, a full spectrum of minerals, and various enzymes. Refrigerate and use within four days.

Cruciferous Veggies

From broccoli and cauliflower to Brussels sprouts, kale, cabbage, and bok choy, the members of the cruciferous or cabbage family pack a nutritional wallop. They contain phytochemicals, vitamins, minerals, and fiber that are important to your health. Studies show that sulforaphane—one of the phytochemicals found in cruciferous vegetables—stimulates enzymes in the body that detoxify carcinogens before they damage cells.

Here's a rundown of the most delicious and nutritious root crops:

- **Broccoli.** Packed with fiber to help regularity, broccoli is also surprisingly high in protein, and it's packed with calcium, antioxidants, and vitamins B6, C, and E. Because of its strong flavor, broccoli works best combined with other vegetables. Wash well and use within four days to get maximum nutrients.

- **Cabbage.** Another member of the fiber-filled cruciferous family, cabbage comes in many different varieties, from white cabbage, which also comes in red and green, to Savoy cabbage, with delicate, crinkly leaves. Other members of the cabbage family you can use in your smoothies include kale, collard greens, Brussels sprouts, and Chinese cabbage. All have large stores of vitamins B6 and C. Kale and collard greens also have a lot of vitamin A and calcium. Members of the cabbage family are also packed with minerals.
- **Cauliflower.** Like other cruciferous vegetables, because of its strong flavor, cauliflower works best as a contributing player rather than a solo act. High in vitamin C and fiber, it has a more delicate taste than other cruciferous veggies. Use within four days or refrigerate for up to a week.

Root Vegetables

Classified by their fleshy underground storage unit or root, which is a holding tank of nutrients, root vegetables are low in fat and high in natural sugars and fiber. Root veggies are also the perfect foods to eat when you need sustained energy and focus.

Powerhouse Veggies

Some of the most nutritious root veggies include those with orangey skins, including carrots, squash, and sweet potatoes. The orange skin signifies they contain beta-carotene, a powerful antioxidant that fights damaging free radicals.

Here are some delicious and nutritious root vegetables to include in your smoothies:

- **Beets.** Both the beet greens and beetroots are blendable and highly nutritious. The roots are packed with calcium, potassium, and vitamins A and C. Choose small to medium beets with fresh green leaves and roots. Use greens within two days and beets within two weeks.
- **Carrots.** Carrots lend a mild, sweet taste to smoothies and taste equally delicious on their own. Carrots are packed with vitamins A, B,

C, D, E, and K, as well as calcium, phosphorous, potassium, sodium, and trace minerals. Carrots stimulate digestion; improve hair, skin, and nails; have a mild diuretic effect; and cleanse the liver, helping to release bile and excess fats. Remove foliage when you get home, because it drains moisture and nutrients from the carrots. Refrigerate and use within a week.

- **Celery.** High in vitamin C and potassium with natural sodium, celery has a mild flavor that blends well with other veggies. Its natural sodium balances the pH of the blood and helps the body use calcium better. Choose firm, bright-green stalks with fresh green leaves. Refrigerate for up to a week.

- **Fennel.** Similar to celery in nutrients and high in sodium, calcium, and magnesium, fennel has a licorice-like taste that enhances the taste of juices made from vegetables with a strong flavor. Choose fennel bulbs the size of tennis balls with no bruising or discoloration. Refrigerate and use within five days.

- **Garlic.** A member of the lily family, this aromatic bulb, high in antioxidants for reducing cholesterol and heart disease, adds flavor and tang. Use one or two cloves per quart. Choose firm, smooth heads and store in a cool, dry place. Use within two weeks.

- **Ginger.** Technically a rhizome and native to Asia, ginger has a sweet, peppery flavor that enhances juice. Buy large, firm nodules with shiny skin. Refrigerate and use within a week.

- **Parsnips.** Cousins to the carrot, parsnips are packed with vitamin C, potassium, silicon, and phosphorous. Choose large, firm parsnips with feathery foliage. Refrigerate and use within a week.

- **Potatoes.** High in vitamins C and B and potassium, potatoes add a light flavor to smoothies. Store in a cool, dry place and use within two weeks.

- **Radishes.** Small but mighty in taste and loaded with vitamin C, iron, magnesium, and potassium, radish juice cleanses the nasal sinuses and gastrointestinal tract and helps clear up skin disorders. Use a handful to add zing. Refrigerate and use within a week.

- **Turnips and turnip greens.** Ounce for ounce, turnip greens have more calcium than milk. The root supplies calcium, potassium, and magnesium. Together, they neutralize overly acidic blood and strengthen bones, hair, nails, and teeth. Store turnips at room temperature, scrub well, and use within two weeks. Refrigerate greens and use within a week.

- **Sweet potatoes and yams.** High in beta-carotene, vitamin C, calcium, and potassium, these two vegetables have a similar taste and can be substituted for one another in recipes. Store in a cool, dry place.
- **Green onions.** Green onions are high in disease-fighting antioxidants and have the mildest flavor of the onion family, making them ideal for blending. They also have antibacterial properties that fight infections and skin diseases. Green onions should be firm and deep green in color. Refrigerate, and use within a week.

Veggies from the Vine

From acorn squash to zucchini, vegetables straight from the vine deliver a cornucopia of nutrients and fiber. Vine vegetables are also especially easy to grow in small, compact gardens or in containers on patios.

- **Cucumbers.** With their mild flavor, cukes complement other vegetables and go well with herbs. Cucumbers are high in vitamin A and silica, which help repair connective tissue and skin. Buy firm, dark-green cucumbers with a slightly bumpy skin. Use within four days.
- **String beans.** High in vitamin B, calcium, magnesium, potassium, protein, and sulfur, string beans are good for your overall metabolism as well as your hair, skin, and nails. They have a strong flavor and taste best when combined with other vegetables.
- **Summer squash and zucchini.** Rich in vitamins B and niacin, calcium, and potassium, summer squash has a bland flavor that works best with other vegetables. It helps cleanse and soothe the bladder and kidneys. Store in a cool, dry place. Use within a few weeks.
- **Tomatoes.** Tomatoes are a good source of lycopene, which has been proven to have anticancer properties, and vitamin C and potassium, which cleanse the liver and add to the body's store of minerals, especially calcium. Fresh tomato juice also stimulates circulation. Store at room temperature.

- **Bell peppers.** High in vitamin C, red peppers are also high in vitamin A and are much sweeter than the green variety. Peppers contribute to beautiful skin and hair, while red peppers stimulate circulation and tone and cleanse the arteries and heart muscle. Store at room temperature. Before blending, wash gently with a mild castile soap, pull out the large clump of seeds, and remove the cap.

Berries

Red, blue, purple, or black—no matter what the color or size, berries are wonder foods that are loaded with phytochemicals, antioxidants, and other vitamins and minerals that help prevent cancer and many other diseases. Cranberries and blueberries also contain a substance that may prevent bladder infections.

FACT

Eating a diet rich in blackberries, blueberries, raspberries, cranberries, and strawberries may help reduce your risk of several types of cancer. The blue color in blueberries comes from anthocyanins, phytochemicals that help protect your body from cancer. Blueberries and raspberries also contain lutein, which is important for healthy vision.

- **Cranberries.** High in vitamin C, B complex, A, and folic acid, cranberries help prevent bladder infections by keeping bacteria from clinging to the wall of the bladder. Cranberries help reduce asthma symptoms, diarrhea, fever, fluid retention, and skin disorders, as well as disorders of the kidney, urinary tract, and lungs. Cranberries also facilitate weight loss.
- **Blueberries and blackberries.** Both berries are packed with sapronins, which improve heart health, as well as disease-fighting antioxidants, vitamin C, minerals, and phytochemicals.
- **Raspberries.** Raspberries are packed with vitamin C and potassium, and are 64 calories per cup.
- **Strawberries.** Strawberries are packed with vitamin C, iron, calcium, magnesium, folate, and potassium—essential for immune-system

function and for strong connective tissue. Strawberries also provide just 53 calories a cup.

FACT

The vitamin C, acidity, and tannins specifically found in cranberries and blueberries have been found to be the main source of protection in the urinary tract from the E. coli bacteria that can build up, causing a urinary tract infection (UTI). By consuming the purest forms of these two berries, the causes and symptoms of a UTI can be alleviated, contributing to the clearing of the infection.

Tree and Vine Fruits

From apples to watermelon, fruits of the tree and vine provide an abundance of life-enhancing and disease-fighting vitamins, minerals, antioxidants, and phytochemicals.

Fruits of the Tree

Tree fruits are as American as apple pie, and are a highly versatile player in making green smoothies, contributing a wide range of flavors, colors, and textures. Here are some of the most popular fruits:

- **Apples.** Rich in vitamins A, B1, B2, B6, and C, folic acid, biotin, and a host of minerals that promote healthy skin, hair, and nails, apples also contain pectin, a fiber that absorbs toxins, stimulates digestion, and helps reduce cholesterol. Apples are extremely versatile and blend well with other juices.
- **Apricots.** Apricots are high in beta-carotene and vitamin A and are a good source of fiber and potassium.
- **Cherries.** Rich in vitamins A, B, and C, folic acid, niacin, and minerals, cherries are potent alkalizers that reduce the acidity of the blood, making them effective in reducing gout, arthritis, and prostate disorders.
- **Grapefruit.** Rich in vitamin C, calcium, phosphorous, and potassium, the pink and red varieties of grapefruit are sweeter and less acidic

than white grapefruit. Grapefruit helps strengthen capillary walls, heal bruising, and reduce skin infections, ear disorders, fever, indigestion, scurvy, varicose veins, obesity, and morning sickness.

- **Lemons.** Lemons are high in citric acid and vitamin C, so a little goes a long way in juicing. Their high antioxidant content and antibacterial properties relieve colds, sore throats, and skin infections and also help reduce anemia, blood disorders, constipation, ear disorders, gout, indigestion, scurvy, skin infections, and obesity.

- **Oranges.** A rich source of vitamins C, B, and K, biotin, folic acid, amino acids, and minerals, oranges cleanse the gastrointestinal tract, strengthen capillary walls, and benefit the heart and lungs. Oranges help reduce anemia, blood disorders, colds, fever, heart disease, high blood pressure, liver disorders, lung disorders, skin disorders, pneumonia, rheumatism, scurvy, and obesity.

- **Limes.** Similar to lemons in nutrients but not as acidic or cleansing, limes can be substituted for lemons in juice recipes.

- **Peaches and nectarines.** High in beta-carotene and vitamins B and C, niacin, and minerals, peaches and nectarines cleanse the intestines and help relieve morning sickness.

- **Pears.** Rich in fiber and vitamins C and B, folic acid, niacin, and the minerals phosphorous and calcium, pears help reduce disorders of the bladder, liver, and prostate as well as constipation.

- **Plums.** High in vitamins C and A, copper, and iron, the benzoic and quinic acids in plums are effective laxatives. Plums help with anemia, constipation, and weight loss.

- **Grapes.** High in caffeic acid, which helps fight cancer, grapes are also packed with bioflavonoids, which help the body absorb vitamin C. Grapes also contain resveratrol, a nutrient that helps prevent liver, lung, breast, and prostate cancer, and saponins, a nutrient that binds with cholesterol and prevents the body from absorbing it.

ESSENTIAL

Rich in fiber, beta-carotene, and sorbitol (a stool-loosening agent), prunes are well respected for their antiaging properties for the body and mind, helping with anemia, improving circulation, and (obviously) resolving constipation issues.

Melons

Melons are the juiciest fruit by far, and naturals for fresh smoothies. They come in many varieties, including canary, cantaloupe, casba, Crenshaw, honeydew, and mush. They are sweet and fun summertime thirst quenchers.

All varieties are rich in vitamins A, B complex, and C and promote skin and nerve health. Melons provide enzymes and natural unconcentrated sugars that help aid digestion.

Best Melons for Smoothies

Cantaloupe, honeydew, and watermelon are among the most popular melons in the United States.

- **Cantaloupe** is high in beta-carotene, vitamin C, and potassium. It alleviates disorders of the bladder, kidney, and skin and reduces constipation.
- **Honeydew** is high in potassium and vitamin C. When blended into smoothies, it promotes energy. It alleviates disorders of the bladder, kidney, and skin and reduces constipation.
- **Watermelon** is high in electrolytes and rich in vitamin A and the mineral potassium. It quenches thirst and also helps cleanse the kidney and bladder. Watermelon helps reduce discomfort associated with aging, arthritis, bladder disorders, constipation, fluid retention, kidney disorders, pregnancy, prostate problems, and skin disorders and promotes weight loss.

Tropical Fruit

You can find a bounty of tropical fruit in your local supermarket, even if you live in a cold climate, including:

- **Avocados.** Although frequently mistaken for a vegetable, the avocado is actually a member of the pear family. Avocados are rich in vitamins A, C, and E. Ripe avocados can be refrigerated for up to five days.
- **Bananas.** Bananas are a great source of potassium, an essential electrolyte, as well as magnesium and vitamin B6.

- **Kiwifruit.** Kiwi are rich in vitamins A and C and contain nearly as much potassium as bananas. Their fuzzy skins contain valuable anti-oxidants and can also be used in marinades for tenderizing meats.
- **Mangos.** Like other orange-colored produce, mangos are packed with beta-carotene.
- **Papayas.** Papayas are loaded with papain, an enzyme that promotes digestion and has been shown to protect the stomach from ulcers. Papayas are also rich in vitamins A and C, and have an abundance of natural sugars. Papayas can also help reduce acidosis, acne, heart disease, tumors, ulcers, and blood disorders.
- **Pineapple.** A great source of potassium, calcium, iron, and iodine, fresh pineapple is worth the hassle required to prepare it for smoothies. Using a strong knife, slice off the top and bottom of the pineapple so it sits flat on your cutting board, and then slice off the peel.

Other Additions

You can boost the taste and nutritional value of your green smoothies with supplements that include soy and nutritional powders and herbal additions.

Best Soy and Powder Additives

Soy and powders can give your smoothies a rich, flavorful taste and texture and boost the nutrient value. They include:

- **Silken tofu**, a soy product, adds flavor and texture and is rich in isoflavones, which may prevent cancer and osteoporosis and help reduce heart disease.
- **Flaxseed** is high in omega-3 acids found in oily fish as well as lecithin, which facilitates digestion.
- **Wheat germ**, high in vitamin E, thiamine, and copper, adds protein and fiber to juice.
- **Bee pollen** is high in protein; vitamins A, B, C, and E; calcium; and magnesium.

Best Herbal Helpers

Herbs lend phytochemicals and fresh taste and aroma to smoothies.

- **Basil** provides vitamins C and A plus beta-carotene.
- **Chives** provide calcium, phosphorous, and several vitamins.
- **Cilantro** is renowned for its anticholesterol, antidiabetic, and anti-inflammatory effects.
- **Dill** is rich in antioxidants and dietary fibers that help control blood cholesterol levels.
- **Mint**, including peppermint and spearmint, has the ability to cut off the blood supply to cancer tumors.
- **Oregano** is among the best sources of vitamin K, and it has antioxidants that prevent cellular damage caused by oxidation of free radicals.
- **Rosemary** provides carnosic acid, which shields the brain from free radicals and lowers the risk of stroke and neurodegenerative diseases.
- **Tarragon** is packed with minerals and vitamins C, B6, A, and E, and may help transfer nutrients to your muscles.

Milk and Yogurt Additions

There are a variety of dairy and nondairy products you can add to your green smoothies to create a delicious, creamy consistency. Some of the most popular additions include:

- **Coconut milk**. Although most people assume coconut milk is the water drained from the coconut, coconut milk is actually derived from the flesh of the coconut. Not only is coconut milk known for its antiviral, antibacterial, and anticarcinogenic properties, it contains a healthy type of easily metabolized saturated fat that is also found in breast milk and is known to promote healthy brain and bone development.

FACT

Coconuts have saved countless lives! During World War II, blood shortages were resolved by doctors using the coconut water from young, green coconuts. Because coconut water has the same electrolyte balance as blood, it was found to be the perfect substitute for blood plasma.

- **Soymilk.** The FDA, American Heart Association, and the American Cancer Society all promote soymilk as a healthy part of a balanced diet. Containing various anticarcinogens, soymilk has been shown to promote health by preventing breast and prostate cancers, fighting heart disease by reducing bad cholesterol (LDL), reversing bone loss associated with osteoporosis, preventing diabetes and kidney disease, and helping with symptoms related to menopause. When selecting a soymilk, try to find one with a low-sugar content or with more naturally occurring sugars.
- **Almond milk.** Rich in copper, manganese, magnesium, potassium, vitamin E, selenium, and calcium, almond milk offers a strong healthy protein-packed alternative to cow's milk. Using almond milk in a green smoothie will lend a nutty background taste.

ESSENTIAL

If the price or ingredients of store-bought almond milk has you considering creating your own at home, follow these simple directions to create your very own homemade almond milk: grind ¼–½ cup of almonds in coffee grinder until fine, then combine in a blender with a cup of pure water for up to 3 minutes. Strain remaining almond bits using a coffee filter.

- **Rice milk.** Processed from brown rice, rice milk has less protein and more carbohydrates than the other milk alternatives, but boosts the body's natural processes with loads of B1 for vitality; B5 for hair, skin, and nails; B6 and folic acid for promoting the healthy metabolism of protein and carbohydrates; and vitamin E for normalizing reproductive health.

- **Kefir.** Although this is still considered a dairy product, it is an easily digested addition to any smoothie that can even be safely consumed by most people with milk allergies. Toting the vitamins and minerals B1, B12, K, and biotin, kefir (which means "feel good" in Turkish) is well known for promoting digestive health with its beneficial yeast and probiotic bacteria.
- **Greek-style yogurt.** Greek-style yogurt contains an average of 20 grams of protein (compared to the 10 grams in the average yogurt) and has almost half the carbohydrates (9 grams versus 15–17 grams) of other yogurts and can also have half the sodium! Because of the triple-strained process it undergoes to remove the whey and water for its creamy texture, Greek-style yogurt is also much thicker and creamier than other yogurts, without the addition of unhealthy thickening agents.

CHAPTER 3

Breakfast Smoothies

Go Bananas

As a very light-flavored green smoothie, this recipe offers an excellent amount of nutrition with a full 2 cups of spinach and 3 servings of fruit. The liquid ingredient can be changed from filtered water to any of the alternative milks.

INGREDIENTS | YIELDS 1 QUART

2 cups spinach leaves

2 ripe bananas, peeled

1 apple, peeled and cored

1 cup purified water

1. Combine spinach, bananas, apple, and ½ cup water in a blender and blend thoroughly.

2. While blending, add remaining water until desired texture is achieved.

PER 1 CUP SERVING: Calories: 75 | Fat: 0g | Protein: 1g | Sodium: 14mg | Fiber: 2g | Carbohydrates: 19g

Carrot Top of the Morning to You

Rich in beta-carotene, this smoothie blends romaine lettuce with tasty carrots and apples to give you a sweet start that can help you stay focused, provide lasting energy, and maintain healthy eyes and metabolism.

INGREDIENTS | YIELDS 1 QUART

2 cups romaine lettuce

3 carrots, peeled and cut into sticks suitable for blender's ability

1 apple, peeled and cored

1 cup purified water

1. Combine first 3 ingredients in the order listed into a blender.

2. Add water slowly while blending until desired texture is achieved.

PER 1 CUP SERVING: Calories: 42 | Fat: 0g | Protein: 1g | Sodium: 35mg | Fiber: 2g | Carbohydrates: 10g

An Apple Pie Day

The cloves and cinnamon in this smoothie add a flavor reminiscent of apple pie and add to the health benefits already present in the spinach, apples, and coconut milk. The fiber alone can help your body feel regular and well-adjusted throughout the day!

INGREDIENTS | YIELDS 1 QUART

2 cups spinach

1 teaspoon cloves

1 teaspoon cinnamon

3 apples, peeled and cored

1½ cups coconut milk

1. Layer the spinach in the blender's container.

2. Add the spices, followed by the apples.

3. Add milk slowly while blending until desired texture is achieved.

PER 1 CUP SERVING: Calories: 232 | Fat: 18g | Protein: 3g | Sodium: 24mg | Fiber: 2g | Carbohydrates: 19g

The Surprising Power of Cloves

Although most consider cloves an essential when it comes time to make pies for the holidays, Ayurvedic healers utilize this spice for its healing powers—it's believed to alleviate symptoms of irregular digestion and malfunctioning metabolism. Although it is used in only small amounts, it's antibacterial and antiviral properties in any amount can't hurt!

A Berry Great Morning

This smoothie is packed with rich antioxidants, powerful phytochemicals, and loads of protein that will get you moving and keep you moving!

INGREDIENTS | YIELDS 1 QUART

2 cups mixed baby greens

1 pint raspberries

1 pint blueberries

1 banana, peeled

1 cup vanilla soymilk

Blueberries and Raspberries for a Healthy Life

Combining raspberries and blueberries in the same smoothie gives your immune system a boost you'd never expect. The vitamins and phytochemicals that burst from these berries and make their skin the vibrant red and purple are what also fight off the cancers, carcinogens, and mental health risks that you'd rather steer clear of!

1. Combine greens, berries, and banana and blend thoroughly.

2. While blending, add soymilk slowly until desired texture is achieved.

PER 1 CUP SERVING: Calories: 94 | Fat: 2g | Protein: 3g | Sodium: 28mg | Fiber: 6g | Carbohydrates: 19g

Mango Tango

*The fruits in this smoothie offer an incredibly sweet and smooth texture
that evens out the bitterness of the dandelion greens nicely. This fruity blend will leave you
energized and ready to conquer the most hectic morning!*

INGREDIENTS | YIELDS 1 QUART

½ cup dandelion greens
1 cup iceberg lettuce
1 ripe mango, peeled and pit removed
1 cup pineapple, cubed
1 orange, peeled
½ cup purified water

1. Combine dandelion greens, iceberg, mango, pineapple, and orange with ¼ cup water and blend thoroughly.

2. While blending, add remaining water until desired texture is achieved.

PER 1 CUP SERVING: Calories: 79 | Fat: 0g | Protein: 1g | Sodium: 9mg | Fiber: 2g | Carbohydrates: 20g

Orange You Glad You Got Up for This?

*Packed with brain-stimulating and immune-protecting vitamin C,
this smoothie is a great option when everyone around you seems to be sick.
Its power is intensified with the antioxidant-rich coconut milk.*

INGREDIENTS | YIELDS 1 QUART

1 cup iceberg lettuce
3 oranges, peeled
½ cup coconut milk

1. Blend iceberg and oranges until just combined.

2. Add coconut milk slowly while blending until desired consistency is reached.

PER 1 CUP SERVING: Calories: 123 | Fat: 6g | Protein: 2g | Sodium: 5mg | Fiber: 4g | Carbohydrates: 18g

Vitamin C

Oranges are well-known for their immunity-building power, and rightfully so! By consuming oranges every day, the human body can fight off illnesses from the common cold to serious cancers and heart disease. You can thank the rich beta-carotenes and the vitamin C. An orange is a definite for health and longevity.

Great Grapefruit

*The grapefruit and cucumber combine in this smoothie to offer
a refreshing zing to your morning with vitamins and nutrients that will
wake you up and keep you feeling fresh throughout the day!*

INGREDIENTS | YIELDS: 1 QUART

1 cup baby greens

2 grapefruits, peeled

1 cucumber, peeled and sliced

¼ cup purified water

1. Combine greens, grapefruit, and cucumber with half of the water and blend.

2. Add remaining water slowly while blending until desired consistency is reached.

PER 1 CUP SERVING: Calories: 59 | Fat: 0g | Protein: 1g | Sodium: 3mg | Fiber: 2g | Carbohydrates: 14g

Splendid Citrus

*Booming with the strong flavors of pineapple, orange, grapefruit,
lemon, and lime, this sweet and tart smoothie will liven your senses while
providing you with a boost in physical and mental health.*

INGREDIENTS | YIELDS 1 QUART

2 large kale leaves

1 cup pineapple, peeled and cubed

1 large orange or 2 small oranges, peeled

1 grapefruit, peeled

½ lemon, peeled

½ lime, peeled

1. Combine kale and all fruits in a blender in the order listed.

2. Blend until desired consistency is reached.

PER 1 CUP SERVING: Calories: 73 | Fat: 0g | Protein: 2g | Sodium: 8mg | Fiber: 3g | Carbohydrates: 18g

Raspberry Tart Morning Start

Raspberries and lime join to make a sweet and tart smoothie that will open your sinuses and sweeten your morning. This blend will please all of your taste buds!

INGREDIENTS | YIELDS 3 CUPS

1 cup Greek-style yogurt
1 cup romaine lettuce
2 pints raspberries
½ lime, peeled

Fight Cancer with Sweetness

With each providing a sweet and tart flavor, limes and raspberries are extremely powerful additions to any day. Rich in antioxidants and packing powerful anticancer properties, these two fruits pair up to keep your immune system running at its best.

1. Pour ½ cup yogurt in a blender, followed by the romaine, raspberries, and lime. Blend.

2. Continue adding remaining yogurt while blending until desired texture is achieved.

PER 1 CUP SERVING: Calories: 118 | Fat: 1g | Protein: 8g | Sodium: 26mg | Fiber: 11g | Carbohydrates: 22g

Coconut Craziness

Adding the flesh of the coconut and the coconut milk to this smoothie results in a sweet flavor that complements the iceberg nicely. This smoothie will make you crave coconuts like crazy!

INGREDIENTS | YIELDS 3–4 CUPS

1 cup iceberg lettuce
Flesh of 2 coconuts
1 cup coconut milk

Coconut Power

In addition to being a staple in the diets of many countries around the world, Western civilizations hold the coconut in a very high regard for its medicinal abilities. Thought to cure and relieve the symptoms associated with many illnesses, the coconut, its flesh, its milk, and the oil that it can produce are packed with intense antioxidants and important vitamins and minerals.

1. Combine iceberg, coconut flesh, and ½ cup coconut milk in a blender, and blend.

2. Add remaining coconut milk while blending until desired texture is achieved.

PER 1 CUP SERVING: Calories: 172 | Fat: 15g | Protein: 2g | Sodium: 9mg | Fiber: 1g | Carbohydrates: 10g

Go Nutty!

Protein, protein, protein! In addition to the vitamins, minerals, and nutrients from the iceberg and banana, the protein from the almond milk and Greek-style yogurt make this smoothie a powerful start to any day.

INGREDIENTS | YIELDS 4 CUPS

½ cup Greek-style yogurt

1 cup iceberg lettuce

1 banana, peeled

1 cup vanilla-flavored almond milk

Make Your Own Almond Milk

Although there are a number of almond milks on the market, some people choose to create their own lower-cost, lower-sugar version at home. If you'd like to create your own almond milk, combine ½ cup water and 1 cup almonds and blend thoroughly. Strain before using.

1. Combine yogurt, iceberg, and banana in a blender with ½ cup of almond milk and blend thoroughly.

2. Continue adding remaining almond milk while blending until desired consistency is reached.

PER 1 CUP SERVING: Calories: 68 | Fat: 1g | Protein: 4g | Sodium: 51mg | Fiber: 1g | Carbohydrates: 12g

Strawberry Start

If you love strawberries, you'll be happy to enjoy one of your favorite fruits while also fulfilling your daily requirement for an entire serving of greens. Agave nectar comes into this smoothie to sweeten the flavor, but only if needed.

INGREDIENTS | YIELDS 3–4 CUPS

½ cup dandelion greens

2 pints strawberries

1 cup vanilla soymilk

1 tablespoon agave nectar, to taste (optional)

Strawberries for Sight

Rich in the antioxidants that give them their vibrant red color, this sweet berry is also rich in vitamins A, C, D, and E, B vitamins, folate, and phytochemicals that join forces to help you maintain healthy eyes and strong vision. Strawberries may help delay the onset of macular degeneration.

1. Add dandelion greens, strawberries, and ½ cup soymilk in a blender and blend until combined.

2. Slowly add remaining ½ cup soymilk while blending until desired consistency is achieved.

3. Stop blending periodically to check for desired sweetness, and drizzle in agave nectar until desired sweetness is achieved.

PER 1 CUP SERVING: Calories: 85 | Fat: 1g | Protein: 3g | Sodium: 31mg | Fiber: 4g | Carbohydrates: 17g

Luscious Lemon-Lime

The tartness of lemons and limes is cooled off with crisp romaine and sweet agave nectar.
The kefir gives a creamy texture with protein and essential vitamins.
The ingredients combine in a delicious smoothie that will make you feel awake and refreshed.

INGREDIENTS | YIELDS 2–3 CUPS

1 cup romaine lettuce
2 lemons, peeled
2 limes, peeled
½ cup kefir
1 tablespoon agave nectar

1. Combine romaine, lemons, limes, and kefir and blend until thoroughly combined.

2. Add agave nectar slowly while blending, stopping periodically to taste, until desired sweetness and texture is achieved.

PER 1 CUP SERVING: Calories: 111 | Fat: 2g | Protein: 3g | Sodium: 36mg | Fiber: 5g | Carbohydrates: 17g

Balance Your Body

Not only do lemons and limes have the acidity and tang to make you pucker up, they are incredibly healthy, too. Those same small, sour fruits that can bring a tear to your eye actually promote a balanced alkaline level in your body.

Delicious Dandelion

A little-known green, the dandelion has been written off as a nuisance or weed.
Although they can be quite bitter, the sweetness from the grapes, apple,
and vanilla soy milk give this smoothie a very different taste that you're sure to enjoy!

INGREDIENTS | YIELDS 3 CUPS

1 cup dandelion greens
1 cup purple seedless grapes
1 sweet apple
1 cup vanilla soymilk

1. Place dandelion greens, grapes, apple, and ½ cup soymilk in the blender and blend until thoroughly combined.

2. Add remaining soymilk while blending until desired texture is achieved.

PER 1 CUP SERVING: Calories: 108 | Fat: 1g | Protein: 3g | Sodium: 47mg | Fiber: 3g | Carbohydrates: 23g

Benefits of Grapes

Although many people choose grapes as a snack because they're a low-calorie and sweet treat, the health benefits of grapes are a great reason to include them in your daily diet. Grapes contain powerful polyphenols that can help reduce the risk of heart disease and fight multiple types of cancer.

The Green Go-Getter

*Packed with green spinach and apples, this creamy green smoothie
will kick your morning off with a boost of essential amino acids,
vitamins, minerals, and an absolutely amazing taste.*

INGREDIENTS | YIELDS 3–4 CUPS

1 cup spinach

2 green apples, peeled and cored

1 banana, peeled

1 cup purified water

1. Place spinach, apples, and banana with ½ cup of water in a blender and blend until thoroughly combined.

2. Continue adding remaining water while blending until desired texture is achieved.

PER 1 CUP SERVING: Calories: 89 | Fat: 0g | Protein: 1g | Sodium: 10mg | Fiber: 3g | Carbohydrates: 23g

A Smoothie for Even the Greenest Green Smoothie Maker!

Some people who are new to creating green smoothies can have a hard time enjoying the powerful taste of the greens. The combination of bananas, apples, and spinach with more fruit than greens provides an appetizing taste that is more sweet and lessens the intensity of the spinach. This smoothie is a great starter for anyone who is turned off by the overpowering taste of greens.

Pear Splendor

Pears give this smoothie its unique sweetness and taste while the banana adds a sweet, smooth texture. Packed with vitamins and nutrients, this smoothie is a sweet and tasty fiber-filled delight!

INGREDIENTS | YIELDS 3 CUPS

1 cup spinach
2 pears, cored and peeled
1 banana, peeled
1 cup almond milk

1. Combine spinach, pears, banana, and ½ cup almond milk in a blender and blend until smooth.

2. While blending, continue adding remaining almond milk until desired texture is achieved.

PER 1 CUP SERVING: Calories: 136 | Fat: 1g | Protein: 1g | Sodium: 59mg | Fiber: 5g | Carbohydrates: 33g

A Sweet Beet to Step To

This deep-purple treat gets its color from the vibrant beets and deep-colored radicchio. Packed with vitamins A, B, C, E, and K, this already nutritious blend packs a protein punch as well with the creamy Greek-style yogurt.

INGREDIENTS | YIELDS 2–3 CUPS

1 cup radicchio
3 cups sliced beets
1 cup Greek-style yogurt

1. Place the radicchio, beets, and ½ cup Greek-style yogurt in a blender and blend to combine thoroughly.

2. While blending, add remaining ½ cup yogurt until desired texture is achieved.

PER 1 CUP SERVING: Calories: 157 | Fat: 0g | Protein: 15g | Sodium: 211mg | Fiber: 6g | Carbohydrates: 25g

Beets' Reddening Effects

If you are new to consuming beets, you should know that you will see some reddening in the smoothie, and more than you would expect. Although not a cause for concern, following beet consumption, urine may turn a slightly reddish or light-purple color, most often found in people with deficient or excess amounts of iron.

Pleasantly Pear

With the variety of fruits coupled with romaine, this smoothie packs whopping amount of vitamins, minerals, and antioxidants, providing your body with unsurpassed nutrition.

INGREDIENTS | YIELDS 3–4 CUPS

1 cup romaine lettuce

2 pears, peeled and cored

1 apple, peeled and cored

1 banana, peeled

½ cup purified water

1. Combine romaine, pears, apple, banana, and ¼ cup water in a blender and blend thoroughly.

2. While blending, add remaining water until desired texture is achieved.

PER 1 CUP SERVING: Calories: 132 | Fat: 0g | Protein: 1g | Sodium: 4mg | Fiber: 6g | Carbohydrates: 35g

Fiber Effects of Pears

Fiber helps keep your digestive tract functioning optimally. Why not enjoy a green smoothie that packs a whopping amount of fiber from greens, pears, and apples? This delicious smoothie can get your digestive system working at its full potential and make irregularity a thing of the past.

Ginger and Spice Make Everything Nice

*This smoothie is packed with the delicious sweet and spicy flavor of ginger
and the amazingly powerful taste of cloves. In combination with the vitamin-rich baby greens
and potassium-packed banana, your morning will be off to a great start!*

INGREDIENTS | YIELDS 3–4 CUPS

1 large nodule ginger, peeled and sliced
¾ cup almond milk
1 teaspoon cloves
1 cup baby greens
1 banana, peeled

Unharness the Power of Ginger

Ayurvedic health practitioners use ginger root as a treatment for an astounding number of ailments. By including ginger with greens and banana, the phytochemicals and antioxidants in this smoothie are powerful in boosting immunity, deterring health risks, and improving the natural functions of body processes.

1. Place the ginger slices and half of the almond milk in a blender and combine thoroughly.

2. Once ginger has thickened the almond milk, add the cloves, baby greens, and banana.

3. While blending, add remaining almond milk until desired texture is achieved.

PER 1 CUP SERVING: Calories: 64 | Fat: 1g | Protein: 1g | Sodium: 42mg | Fiber: 2g | Carbohydrates: 14g

Mango Madness

The color of this smoothie is vibrant, and the beta-carotene, vitamins A and E, and strong variety of minerals found in it help strengthen your bones and eyes.

INGREDIENTS | YIELDS 3–4 CUPS

½ cup dandelion greens

½ cup romaine lettuce

2 mangoes, peeled and pit removed

1 banana, peeled

½ cup purified water

1. Place dandelion greens, romaine, mangoes, banana, and half of the water in a blender and combine thoroughly.

2. While blending, add remaining water until desired texture is achieved.

PER 1 CUP SERVING: Calories: 130 | Fat: 1g | Protein: 1g | Sodium: 12mg | Fiber: 4g | Carbohydrates: 34g

Everyday Smoothies

Calming Cucumber

*The light taste of cucumber and the powerfully fragrant mint combine
with the deep green romaine in this delightfully smooth and refreshing smoothie.
Not only can this be a great start to your day, it can also be the sweet end of it!*

INGREDIENTS | YIELDS 3–4 CUPS

1 cup romaine lettuce

2 cucumbers, peeled

¼ cup mint, chopped

1 cup purified water

Cucumbers Aren't Just Water

Even though a cucumber is mostly water
(and fiber), it is far more than a tasty,
hydrating, and filling snack option. These
green veggies are a great addition to a diet
in need of moisture and clarity . . . for the
skin! A clear complexion is an aesthetic
benefit of consuming cucumbers. By consuming 1 serving of cucumbers per day,
you'll not only fulfill a full serving of veggies and stave off hunger, you'll have clear,
hydrated skin!

1. Place romaine, cucumbers, mint, and ½ cup water in a
   blender and combine thoroughly.

2. Add remaining water while blending until desired
   texture is achieved.

PER 1 CUP SERVING: Calories: 24 | Fat: 0g | Protein: 1g |
Sodium: 9mg | Fiber: 2g | Carbohydrates: 4g

Splendid Melon

*While endive is more commonly found in salads or as a garnish,
this green is a wonderful base to this smoothie. The cantaloupe and honeydew melon
add sweet nectar that will quench any need your body may have.*

INGREDIENTS | YIELDS 3–4 CUPS

1 cup endive

1 cantaloupe, peeled and seeds removed

1 honeydew, peeled and seeds removed

½ cup ice cubes (optional)

1. Combine endive, cantaloupe, and honeydew in a blender and blend thoroughly until desired texture is achieved.

2. If a thicker consistency is desired, ice can be added while blending until desired consistency is reached.

PER 1 CUP SERVING: Calories: 185 | Fat: 1g | Protein: 4g | Sodium: 93mg | Fiber: 5g | Carbohydrates: 47g

Cantaloupe Promotes Energy

In a single serving of cantaloupe, there are a variety of vitamins and minerals that promote great health, including over 100 percent of the Recommended Daily Amount (RDA) of vitamins C and A. One of the most astounding benefits of this fruit is its major role in promoting metabolism, more specifically, the metabolism of carbohydrates.

Tempting Tomato

The sweet yet tangy twist that results from the combination of the tomatoes, celery, peas, and cabbage can be an inviting savory treat enjoyed morning, noon, or night.

INGREDIENTS | YIELDS 3–4 CUPS

1 cup cabbage

2 tomatoes, skin intact

1 celery stalk

½ cup sweet peas

½ cup purified water

1. Place cabbage, tomatoes, celery, peas, and half of the water in a blender and blend until thoroughly combined.

2. Continue adding remaining water while blending until desired texture is achieved.

PER 1 CUP SERVING: Calories: 44 | Fat: 0g | Protein: 3g | Sodium: 22mg | Fiber: 3g | Carbohydrates: 9g

Pass the Peas, Please

There's no veggie easier than the pea! Sweet and refreshing, you can serve them hot or munch on them cold. They require little prep time and taste great in a variety of dishes. This tiny veggie packs a punch in terms of all of the vitamins and nutrients it delivers. One cup of peas provides 50 percent of your daily value of vitamin K, which promotes efficient blood clotting and optimizes bone health while deterring osteoporosis.

Super Celery

This combination of greens and rich vegetables offers a healthy dose of fiber; vitamins A, B, C, and K; and a wealth of minerals like iron and potassium; the best part is, it's absolutely delicious!

INGREDIENTS | YIELDS 3–4 CUPS

1 cup spinach

3 celery stalks

1 cucumber, peeled

1 carrot, peeled

1 cup purified water

Celery and Water Weight

Whether you're male or female, you've felt the "bloat." Sodium, sugar, hormones, stress, diet, fluid intake, and many more factors can lead to an excessive retention of water. In order to beat the bloat, the remedy may be as easy as eating a few celery stalks! The potassium, sodium, and fiber in celery combine to effectively fight water retention.

1. Place spinach, celery, cucumber, carrot, and ½ cup water in a blender and blend until thoroughly combined.

2. Continue adding remaining water as you blend until desired texture is achieved.

PER 1 CUP SERVING: Calories: 34 | Fat: 0g | Protein: 1g | Sodium: 72mg | Fiber: 3g | Carbohydrates: 7g

Very Veggie

Spinach acts as the green base to this smoothie with the plentiful colors and tastes coming from the addition of carrots, celery, tomato, green onion, and parsley.

INGREDIENTS | YIELDS 3–4 CUPS

1 cup spinach

2 celery stalks

2 carrots, peeled

1 tomato

1 green onion

1 small sprig parsley (optional)

1 cup purified water

1. Place the spinach, celery, carrots, tomato, green onion, parsley, and ½ cup water in a blender and blend until thoroughly combined.

2. If necessary, continue adding remaining water while blending until desired texture is achieved.

PER 1 CUP SERVING: Calories: 32 | Fat: 0g | Protein: 1g | Sodium: 62mg | Fiber: 2g | Carbohydrates: 7g

The Power of Parsley

That green garnish that arrives as a decoration on the side of your plate is not given the attention it deserves! This green leafy herb is rich in vitamins and minerals. In just 1 serving of this cleansing green, there are impressive amounts of vitamins K, C, and A as well as iron and folate. By including just 2 tablespoons of parsley in your daily diet, you'll consume more than 153 percent of your needed vitamin K!

Go, Go, Garlic!

Rich in vitamins and minerals and delivering a wide variety of health benefits, garlic is a powerful addition to any diet in need of a boost. It poses a deterrent to illness and disease and aids in the optimal functioning of the body's natural processes.

INGREDIENTS | YIELDS 3–4 CUPS

1 cup romaine lettuce

2 tomatoes

½ cup basil leaves

3 garlic cloves, crushed and let sit for 1 hour

½ cup purified water (if necessary)

1. Place romaine, tomatoes, basil, and garlic in a blender and combine thoroughly until all garlic is emulsified.

2. Add water while blending, if needed, until desired consistency is reached.

PER 1 CUP SERVING: Calories: 23 | Fat: 0g | Protein: 1g | Sodium: 6mg | Fiber: 1g | Carbohydrates: 5g

Garlic at Room Temperature

The amazing cancer-fighting benefits and strong antiviral and antibacterial properties in garlic are maximized when the garlic clove has been crushed and allowed to set at room temperature. Heating garlic cloves inhibits the full ability of important enzymes to do their work. Maximize garlic's full potential by preparing it at room temperature in your green smoothies.

One Superb Herb

Although basil has become more and more common as a main ingredient in things like pesto and pasta sauce, this herb still doesn't get the attention it deserves for the health benefits it offers.

INGREDIENTS | YIELDS 3–4 CUPS

1 cup iceberg lettuce

½ cup basil

1 cucumber, peeled

1 garlic clove

½ cup purified water

1. Place the iceberg, basil, cucumber, and garlic in a blender with half of the water and blend until combined thoroughly.

2. If needed, continue adding remaining water while blending until desired texture is achieved.

PER 1 CUP SERVING: Calories: 14 | Fat: 0g | Protein: 1g | Sodium: 5mg | Fiber: 1g | Carbohydrates: 3g

Basil and Vitamin K

Although the greens blended into green smoothies offer vitamin K, the added benefit of using basil can be quite astounding. While many greens' servings may offer a healthy helping of vitamin K, just 2 teaspoons (or 3 grams) of basil can account for 60 percent of your RDA of vitamin K. You might fulfill, or even surpass, your recommended amount of vitamin K by just mixing the greens and basil in one smoothie!

Minty Madness

Combining mint with iceberg, cucumbers, and rice milk in this smoothie offers the health benefits of vitamins A,C, and K while creating a pleasurable cooling effect in your mouth, body, and mind.

INGREDIENTS | YIELDS 3–4 CUPS

1 cup iceberg lettuce

½ cup mint

1 cucumber, peeled

1 cup rice milk

Mint and Digestion

Mint gums that make your mouth feel clean and your breath taste fresh are not the only great contribution this wonderful herb has given humanity. As an herb with strong antiseptic, antibacterial, and antifungal properties, mint has the ability to calm the stomach and digestive system. Stomach aches, irregularity, and irritable bowel syndrome can all be aided with the use of mint.

1. Place the iceberg, mint, cucumber, and half of the rice milk in a blender and blend until thoroughly combined.

2. If needed, add remaining rice milk while blending until desired consistency is reached.

PER 1 CUP SERVING: Calories: 65 | Fat: 1g | Protein: 2g | Sodium: 46mg | Fiber: 3g | Carbohydrates: 12g

Crazy Carrot

Some may not believe a green vegetable smoothie could be sweet and delicious— this smoothie is one for those nonbelievers. Crisp romaine, sweet carrots, and smooth banana meet in this smoothie to provide a treat for your senses!

INGREDIENTS | YIELDS 3–4 CUPS

1 cup romaine lettuce

3 carrots, peeled

1 banana, peeled

½ cup vanilla or plain almond milk

Carrots, Bananas, and B6

Of all the vitamins carrots and bananas contain, they provide an astounding amount of vitamin B6, heralded for its functions and processes in the body. From skin care to emotional disturbances due to hormone fluctuation (including PMS and menopause), the health benefits of B6 stretch to include protection from heart disease and certain cancers.

1. Place romaine, carrots, banana, and half of the almond milk in a blender and blend until thoroughly combined.

2. If needed, add remaining almond milk while blending until desired consistency is reached.

PER 1 CUP SERVING: Calories: 78 | Fat: 1g | Protein: 1g | Sodium: 69mg | Fiber: 3g | Carbohydrates: 18g

Sublime Lime

The tart taste of lime in this smoothie is balanced nicely with the addition of the sweet and thickening banana, a sweet treat that may give your face a reason to pucker up momentarily!

INGREDIENTS | YIELDS 3–4 CUPS

1 cup spinach

2 limes, peeled and deseeded

1 banana, peeled

½ cup purified water

1. Place spinach, limes, and banana in a blender with half of the water and blend until thoroughly combined.

2. If needed, add remaining water while blending until desired consistency is achieved.

PER 1 CUP SERVING: Calories: 51 | Fat: 0g | Protein: 1g | Sodium: 10mg | Fiber: 2g | Carbohydrates: 14g

Limes and Joints

Although many patients suffering from arthritis decide to exercise and eat differently, few know the powerful effects limes can have on joints! These vitamin C–filled fruits can pack a punch in getting arthritis symptoms to a minimum and making everyday life seem less achy where the limbs bend!

The Hangover Helper

When you realize certain lifestyle choices may not make for the best days following, this smoothie is the perfect pick-me-up to calm your head and your stomach while pleasing your taste buds.

INGREDIENTS | YIELDS 3–4 CUPS

1 cup iceberg lettuce

1 apple, cored and peeled

1 banana, peeled

½"–1" ginger root, peeled and sliced or chopped

1 cup vanilla almond milk

1. Place iceberg, apple, banana, ginger, and half of the almond milk in a blender and blend until thoroughly combined.

2. If needed, add remaining half of almond milk while blending until desired texture is achieved.

PER 1 CUP SERVING: Calories: 103 | Fat: 1g | Protein: 1g | Sodium: 54mg | Fiber: 3g | Carbohydrates: 24g

Ginger and Hangovers

Because the ginger root's capabilities include alleviating symptoms associated with indigestion, nausea, and fever as well as promoting optimal blood circulation and maintaining clear sinuses, this is one ingredient that can help ease many of the symptoms resulting from an evening of too much of anything. This smoothie is a must for any of those not-so-healthy days!

A Bitter-Sweet Treat

*The watercress, carrots, and sweet fruits in this recipe
make for a tantalizing smoothie you won't soon forget!*

INGREDIENTS | YIELDS 3–4 CUPS

1 cup watercress

3 carrots, peeled

2 apples, cored and peeled

1 banana, peeled

1 cup coconut milk

1. Place watercress, carrots, apples, banana, and ½ cup coconut milk in a blender and blend until thoroughly combined.

2. If needed, add remaining ½ cup of coconut milk while blending until desired texture is achieved.

PER 1 CUP SERVING: Calories: 205 | Fat: 12g | Protein: 2g | Sodium: 44mg | Fiber: 4g | Carbohydrates: 25g

Watercress

You may have heard of watercress but never actually tried it. If that's the case, you'll be pleasantly surprised with this smoothie. With a delicious taste, this green (not a lettuce, but a green) is rich in disease- and cancer-fighting properties that will keep your immune system, brain, blood, bones, and even your sex drive running at optimal levels.

Green Gazpacho

*This smoothie is modeled after gazpacho, a delightful cold soup
prepared from a tomato base with onions, cucumber, bell pepper, and garlic.*

INGREDIENTS | YIELDS 3–4 CUPS

1 cup watercress

2 tomatoes

1 cucumber, peeled

1 celery stalk

½ red onion

½ green pepper

3 garlic cloves

1 small jalapeño (optional)

3 tablespoons red wine vinegar

2 tablespoons basil leaves, chopped

1 cup purified water, if needed

1. Place all ingredients except the purified water in a blender and blend until thoroughly combined.

2. If needed, slowly add purified water while blending until desired texture is achieved.

PER 1 CUP SERVING: Calories: 34 | Fat: 0g | Protein: 2g | Sodium: 18mg | Fiber: 2g | Carbohydrates: 7g

A Vegetable Fiesta in Your Blender

This popular vegetable soup is served cold and is absolutely packed with a wide variety of vegetables! Between the watercress, cucumber, celery, tomatoes, onion, peppers, and herbs, there aren't many vitamins and minerals left out in this smoothie. The green color, fresh taste, and zing that can only come from a combination of veggies like these are delivered in this powerfully packed smoothie.

Oh, Sweet Cabbage

As a delightfully sweet morning starter or equally enjoyable afternoon pick-me-up, this smoothie's combination of cabbage, carrots, and apples will have you wondering why you never considered cabbage a treat before.

INGREDIENTS | YIELDS 3–4 CUPS

1 cup cabbage

3 carrots, peeled

1 apple, cored and peeled

1 cup purified water

1. Place cabbage, carrots, and apple with ½ cup water in a blender and blend until thoroughly combined.

2. Add remaining ½ cup water slowly while blending until desired texture is achieved.

PER 1 CUP SERVING: Calories: 48 | Fat: 0g | Protein: 1g | Sodium: 37mg | Fiber: 3g | Carbohydrates: 12g

Cancer-Fighting Cabbage

Although some green, leafy vegetables don't top the list of those liked enough to be included in your daily diet, cabbage is one that certainly deserves some room near the top. With all of the antioxidants that fight cancer-causing free radical damage against cells, even the lightest white cabbage (the most consumed of all cabbages) is rich enough to help stop cancer in its tracks!

Savoy Smoothie

The strong beta-carotenes in this smoothie will help keep you energized and focused throughout the day. Whether you're looking for a great morning start or a quick and healthy lunch idea, this smoothie is a great go-to!

INGREDIENTS | YIELDS 3–4 CUPS

1 cup savoy cabbage

1 beet

1 carrot, peeled

1 apple, cored and peeled

1 banana, peeled

1 cup vanilla soymilk

1. Place the cabbage, beet, carrot, apple, and banana with ½ cup of the soymilk in a blender and blend until thoroughly combined.

2. Add remaining ½ cup of soymilk while blending until desired texture is achieved.

PER 1 CUP SERVING: Calories: 95 | Fat: 1g | Protein: 3g | Sodium: 56mg | Fiber: 4g | Carbohydrates: 20g

Savoy and Vitamin K

Cabbage is packed with vitamin K, whose most well-known benefit is its large responsibility in blood clotting. By consuming just 1 cup of savoy cabbage, you'll be getting more than 90 percent of your RDA of vitamin K.

The Slump Bumper

With the energizing effects of natural sugars (fructose) found in sweet fruits and vegetables, there's no comparison to energy drinks or junk foods that give you quick but short-lived energy.

INGREDIENTS | YIELDS 3–4 CUPS

1 cup spinach
2 pears, cored and peeled
1 cup cherries, pitted
1 banana, peeled
2 cups almond milk

Benefits of Cherries

Packed with an assortment of vitamins and minerals, an obvious sign from their intense red color, cherries help mental functions like memory. Cherries also improve mental clarity and promote focus and attention.

1. Place spinach, pears, cherries, banana, and 1 cup of almond milk in a blender and blend until thoroughly combined.

2. Add remaining cup of almond milk while blending until desired texture is achieved.

PER 1 CUP SERVING: Calories: 149 | Fat: 2g | Protein: 2g | Sodium: 82mg | Fiber: 5g | Carbohydrates: 35g

Beet Booster

Beets, beets, beets! This purple smoothie is not only attractive, it's a delicious way to sneak plenty of fruit and vegetable servings into your diet.

INGREDIENTS | YIELDS 3–4 CUPS

1 cup beet greens
3 beets
1 banana, peeled
2 cups purified water

1. Place beet greens, beets, banana, and 1 cup of water in a blender and blend until thoroughly combined.

2. Add remaining cup of water while blending until desired texture is achieved.

PER 1 CUP SERVING: Calories: 55 | Fat: 0g | Protein: 2g | Sodium: 72mg | Fiber: 3g | Carbohydrates: 13g

Berry, Berry Delicious

The sweet tang of oranges, strawberries, and blueberries combine beautifully with the romaine in this smoothie to develop a deliciously refreshing treat.

INGREDIENTS | YIELDS 3–4 CUPS

1 cup romaine lettuce

2 oranges, peeled

1 cup strawberries

1 cup blueberries

1 cup vanilla almond milk

Citric Acid and Flavor

Lemon, lime, and orange juices are commonly used in foods and drinks with the main purpose of enhancing the flavors of the main ingredient. A small amount of acidic citrus juice can add a depth to the flavors of fruits or vegetables, and the result in smoothies containing berries is an amplified sweetness of the berries' natural flavors.

1. Place the romaine, oranges, berries, and ½ cup of almond milk in a blender and blend until thoroughly combined.

2. Add remaining ½ cup of almond milk while blending until desired texture is achieved.

PER 1 CUP SERVING: Calories: 121 | Fat: 1g | Protein: 2g | Sodium: 40mg | Fiber: 5g | Carbohydrates: 29g

Peachy Berry

If you love peaches and berries, combining them with the baby greens in this smoothie delivers sweet tastes with vitamins and nutrients.

INGREDIENTS | YIELDS 3–4 CUPS

1 cup baby greens
2 peaches, pitted and peeled
1 cup strawberries
1 banana, peeled
½ tablespoon ginger, sliced or grated
Purified water, to taste (optional)

1. Add all ingredients to a blender and blend until thoroughly combined.

2. Add water, if necessary, while blending if smoothie is too thick.

PER 1 CUP SERVING: Calories: 92 | Fat: 1g | Protein: 2g | Sodium: 3mg | Fiber: 4g | Carbohydrates: 23g

Organic Alert!

Although peaches can be found in almost every grocery store and fruit stand during their season as well as year-round in the grocer's freezer, it is an important fruit to purchase organic. Because of its thin flesh, it is more susceptible to the pesticides and preservatives used in the nonorganic growing process. Although more pricey than nonorganic varieties, buying organic peaches is important for your health and your family's.

Apple-Ginger Delight

*The smooth, creamy Greek-style yogurt, apples,
and ginger combine in this recipe for a truly delicious treat. Enjoy!*

INGREDIENTS | YIELDS 3–4 CUPS

1 cup romaine lettuce

2 apples, cored and peeled

½" nodule ginger root, peeled

½ cup Greek-style yogurt

Cravings for Sweets

Everybody is familiar with the common craving. Cravings may vary from person to person—you may crave salty or sweet, for example. Either way, apples have been known to curb most cravings, and also create a feeling of fullness. When a craving hits, eat an apple with a full glass of water and wait 30 minutes. Chances are your craving will have subsided and you will have replaced a higher-calorie option with a nutritious snack!

1. Place romaine, apples, ginger, and half of the yogurt in a blender and blend until thoroughly combined.

2. Add remaining yogurt while blending until desired texture is achieved.

PER 1 CUP SERVING: Calories: 88 | Fat: 0g | Protein: 4g | Sodium: 18mg | Fiber: 3g | Carbohydrates: 19g

Dessert Smoothies

A Sweet Beet Treat

When you're looking for a sweet treat, beets are vitamin- and nutrient-packed vegetables that offer up a sweet taste comparable to many fruits. This recipe is just one of the many greens and beet combinations that you'll enjoy!

INGREDIENTS | YIELDS 3–4 CUPS

1 cup beet greens

3 beets

1 banana, peeled

1 cup almond milk

½ cup ice cubes (optional)

Beet Greens

While the actual beets are what have the reputation for being sweet, nutritious, delicious little veggies, the roots and greens of the beet are also edible and highly nutritious. Packed with calcium, potassium, and vitamins A and C, the roots and leaves of these powerful deep-purple veggies are a healthy addition to any diet.

1. Place beet greens, beets, banana, and ½ cup almond milk in a blender container and blend until thoroughly combined.

2. Add remaining almond milk and ice while blending until desired texture is achieved.

PER 1 CUP SERVING: Calories: 77 | Fat: 1g | Protein: 2g | Sodium: 107mg | Fiber: 3g | Carbohydrates: 17g

Cool Cucumber Melon

The mix of romaine, cucumbers, honeydew, and mint in this recipe
combine beautifully to develop one of the most crisp, refreshing smoothies you'll taste.

INGREDIENTS | YIELDS 3–4 CUPS

1 cup romaine lettuce

1 sprig mint leaves

3 cucumbers, peeled

½ honeydew melon, peeled, seeds removed

½ cup kefir

1. In a blender, place romaine and mint leaves followed by the cucumbers, melon, and half of the kefir and blend until thoroughly combined.

2. Add remaining half of kefir while blending until desired texture is achieved.

PER 1 CUP SERVING: Calories: 86 | Fat: 1g | Protein: 3g | Sodium: 43mg | Fiber: 3g | Carbohydrates: 17g

Cucumbers and Skin

If you're exfoliating, hydrating, and moisturizing your skin but still feel like you're not reaching that desired clarity and glow, try working on your complexion from the *inside*. Packed with the powerful combination of vitamin A and silica, cucumbers can help repair connective tissue and skin. So, instead of buying that new and improved face cream, include a couple of servings of cucumbers for that healthy skin you desire!

A Berry Delicious End to the Day

When the sweetness of a berry smoothie sounds just perfect, treat yourself to this homemade version that offers more health benefits and the peace of mind from knowing exactly how it's made.

INGREDIENTS | YIELDS 3–4 CUPS

1 cup iceberg lettuce

1 pint strawberries

1 pint blueberries

1 banana, peeled

½ cup vanilla almond milk

½ cup ice cubes (optional)

1. Place iceberg, strawberries, blueberries, banana, and almond milk in a blender until thoroughly combined.

2. Add optional ice cubes while blending until desired texture is achieved.

PER 1 CUP SERVING: Calories: 111 | Fat: 1g | Protein: 2g | Sodium: 22mg | Fiber: 5g | Carbohydrates: 27g

Berries and the Bladder

Although many people consider them just tasty fruits, berries are well-known super-foods that can improve health and prevent illness. In addition to contributing to strong heart health, blueberries and cranberries promote bladder health by acting as a guard against E. coli bacteria, which is the culprit in urinary tract infections.

Wacky Watermelon

*Watermelon's amazing taste isn't the only great thing about this fruit.
Packed with vitamins, minerals, nutrients, and a ton of water, you'll be satisfying
your sweet tooth while quenching your thirst at the same time!*

INGREDIENTS | YIELDS 3–4 CUPS

1 cup iceberg lettuce
½ sprig mint leaves
2 cups watermelon
1 cucumber, peeled
Purified water, to taste (optional)

1. Place the iceberg, mint, watermelon, and cucumber in a blender and blend until thoroughly combined.

2. Add additional water, if necessary, while blending until desired texture is achieved.

PER 1 CUP SERVING: Calories: 32 | Fat: 0g | Protein: 1g | Sodium: 4mg | Fiber: 1g | Carbohydrates: 7g

Water-Melon

The average person has a hard time getting the recommended daily 8–10 glasses of water. Whether the flavorless drink is unappealing, sweet and sugary drink alternatives are more desirable, or the actual consumption of 64 ounces seems tedious, hydrating can be difficult. The alternative to drinking your daily water requirement is to consume it through fruits and vegetables that contain a lot of water. With the high water content of the ingredients in this smoothie, you may not even need to add any additional fluid!

Chocolatey Dream

Ahhhh, chocolate! It's pretty difficult to find someone who doesn't like chocolate, and this smoothie has the perfect blend of ingredients to satisfy any chocolate craving.

INGREDIENTS | YIELDS 3–4 CUPS

1 cup watercress

2 tablespoons raw powdered cocoa

2 bananas, peeled

2 cups almond milk

Chocolate Is Healthy?

Chocolate has been determined to be beneficial in the daily diet! Now, don't take this as a go-ahead to dive into that huge bag of M&M's. Powdered, unprocessed cocoa is the chocolate shown to provide the most benefits. Although the candy bar alternative may seem more gratifying, the sugar content, trans fats, and milk products may be the reason they haven't yet been labeled superfoods.

1. In a blender, place the watercress and cocoa powder, followed by the bananas and 1 cup of the almond milk and blend until thoroughly combined.

2. Add remaining cup of almond milk while blending until desired texture is achieved.

PER 1 CUP SERVING: Calories: 104 | Fat: 2g | Protein: 2g | Sodium: 80mg | Fiber: 3g | Carbohydrates: 23g

The Joy of Almonds

If that Almond Joy candy is what satisfies your sweet tooth, this smoothie is for you. Packed with the flavors of almonds and coconut, this creamy smoothie will surely become one of your favorites!

INGREDIENTS | YIELDS 3–4 CUPS

½ cup almonds

2 cups coconut milk

1 cup romaine lettuce

Flesh of 2 mature coconuts

1 banana

1. Combine the almonds and ½ cup of coconut milk in a blender and emulsify until most remnants of the almonds have been liquefied, adding more liquid as needed.

2. Add the romaine, coconut flesh, banana, and 1 cup of coconut milk and blend until thoroughly combined.

3. Add remaining ½ cup of coconut milk, if needed, while blending until desired texture is achieved.

PER 1 CUP SERVING: Calories: 1056 | Fat: 100g | Protein: 13g | Sodium: 56mg | Fiber: 21g | Carbohydrates: 44g

Pumpkin Spice

Who doesn't love the sweet aroma of freshly baked pumpkin pie?
This recipe will be as sweet and tempting as a heaping helping of the not-so-nutritious baked alternative,
but with all of the delicious and nutritious goodness!

INGREDIENTS | YIELDS 3–4 CUPS

½ cup pumpkin, cubed or diced

1 cup vanilla soymilk

1 cup romaine lettuce

1 teaspoon cloves

1 tablespoon ginger, grated

½ cup Greek-style yogurt

The Power of Pumpkin

Rich in vitamins and nutrients, this beta-carotene-rich squash contains a surprising amount of nutrition. Pumpkin contains more than 140 percent of your daily value of vitamin A in just ½ cup. By consuming pumpkin with ginger, yogurt, and soymilk in this smoothie, you'll be getting a protein-packed, vitamin-rich treat that will satisfy your need for pumpkin pie any time of year.

1. Combine pumpkin and ½ cup soymilk in a blender until completely emulsified.

2. Add romaine, cloves, ginger, and yogurt and blend until thoroughly combined.

3. If needed, add remaining soymilk while blending until desired consistency is achieved.

PER 1 CUP SERVING: Calories: 66 | Fat: 1g | Protein: 6g | Sodium: 51mg | Fiber: 1g | Carbohydrates: 7g

Sweet Potato Pie

*This delicious smoothie—with flavors reminiscent of sweet potato pie—
makes a healthy alternative to the real thing, packed with vitamins, minerals, and antioxidants.*

INGREDIENTS | YIELDS 3–4 CUPS

2 sweet potatoes, peeled and cut for blender's ability

2 cups vanilla soymilk

1 teaspoon cloves

½"–1" knob of ginger

1 cup spinach

Sweet Potatoes for Smokers

Smokers can benefit more than nonsmokers from this orange vegetable. Rich in vitamin A, sweet potatoes fight diseases of the lung by reversing vitamin A deficiencies. Research has shown that vitamin A deficiencies actually create a susceptibility to lung diseases in smokers and those regularly exposed to secondhand smoke.

1. Place the sweet potatoes with 1 cup vanilla soymilk in a blender and blend until sweet potato is completely emulsified.

2. Add cloves, ginger, and spinach and blend until thoroughly combined.

3. Add remaining 1 cup of soymilk while blending until desired texture is achieved.

PER 1 CUP SERVING: Calories: 111 | Fat: 2g | Protein: 4g | Sodium: 91mg | Fiber: 3g | Carbohydrates: 19g

Minty Bliss

*The ingredients here blend together to create a sweet treat with a creamy texture; this smoothie
may be satisfying enough to bump your favorite ice cream out of its number one spot!*

INGREDIENTS | YIELDS 3–4 CUPS

1 cup iceberg lettuce

¼ cup whole mint leaves

1 pint raspberries

1 cup almond milk

½ cup Greek-style yogurt

1. Place the iceberg, mint, raspberries, and almond milk in a blender and blend until thoroughly combined.

2. Add yogurt while blending until desired texture is achieved.

PER 1 CUP SERVING: Calories: 86 | Fat: 1g | Protein: 5g | Sodium: 54mg | Fiber: 6g | Carbohydrates: 16g

Coconut Cream Dream

Coconut cream pies are a delicious dessert, but pack empty calories and have little vitamins and minerals. This recipe blends the star ingredients of coconut cream pie in a healthy green smoothie.

INGREDIENTS | YIELDS 3–4 CUPS

1 cup romaine lettuce
Flesh of 2 mature coconuts
1 tablespoon lemon juice
1 banana, peeled
¼" ginger, peeled
½ cup almond milk
½ cup Greek-style yogurt

1. Place romaine, coconut flesh, lemon juice, banana, ginger, and almond milk in a blender and blend until thoroughly combined.

2. Add the yogurt while blending until desired texture is achieved.

PER 1 CUP SERVING: Calories: 760 | Fat: 67g | Protein: 10g | Sodium: 72mg | Fiber: 19g | Carbohydrates: 41g

Sinful Strawberry Cream

When a craving for something sweet and delicious hits, this is a simple go-to you're sure to enjoy. Rich, sweet, and creamy, this recipe will simultaneously satisfy your sweet tooth and your daily value of important vitamins and minerals.

INGREDIENTS | YIELDS 3–4 CUPS

1 cup spinach
2 pints strawberries
1 banana, peeled
1 cup kefir

1. Place spinach, strawberries, banana, and ½ cup kefir in a blender container and blend until thoroughly combined.

2. Add remaining ½ cup kefir while blending until desired texture is achieved.

PER 1 CUP SERVING: Calories: 126 | Fat: 3g | Protein: 4g | Sodium: 39mg | Fiber: 5g | Carbohydrates: 24g

Kefir Versus Milk

If you've never indulged in this awesome milk alternative, now may be the perfect time. Kefir contains a plethora of vitamins, beneficial probiotic bacteria, and rich enzymes that promote healthy growth, optimize digestion, and fight illness. The best part is that almost every grocery store that carries milk products will carry kefir, so the switch is as easy as walking further down the aisle.

Raspberry Delight

This smooth blend of raspberries and banana packs vitamins and minerals into a deliciously sweet dessert. With the added nutrition from the lettuce, rice milk, and yogurt, this smoothie packs protein, iron, folate, and B vitamins galore!

INGREDIENTS | YIELDS 3–4 CUPS

1 cup iceberg lettuce

2 pints raspberries

1 banana, peeled

½ cup rice milk

½ cup Greek-style yogurt

1. Place iceberg, raspberries, banana, and rice milk in a blender and blend until thoroughly combined.

2. Add Greek-style yogurt while blending until desired texture is achieved.

PER 1 CUP SERVING: Calories: 141 | Fat: 1g | Protein: 5g | Sodium: 28mg | Fiber: 11g | Carbohydrates: 30g

Banana Nut Blend

Waking up to the sweet aroma of fresh-baked banana bread can't be replaced . . . until you taste this smoothie!

INGREDIENTS | YIELDS 3–4 CUPS

¼ cup walnuts

1 cup vanilla almond milk

1 cup romaine lettuce

2 bananas, peeled

1. Place walnuts and ½ cup almond milk in a blender and blend until walnuts are completely emulsified.

2. Add romaine, bananas, and remaining ½ cup almond milk while blending until desired texture is achieved.

PER 1 CUP SERVING: Calories: 99 | Fat: 6g | Protein: 2g | Sodium: 39mg | Fiber: 2g | Carbohydrates: 12g

Walnuts and Antioxidants

When you think of antioxidant-rich foods, walnuts probably aren't your first thought, but just ¼ cup of walnuts carries almost 100 percent of your daily value of omega-3 fatty acids, and is loaded with monounsaturated fats. Of the tree nuts, walnuts, chestnuts, and pecans carry the highest amount of antioxidants, which can prevent illness and reverse oxidative damage done by free radicals.

Blueberry Supreme

Blueberries take center stage in this antioxidant-packed, day-brightening recipe!

INGREDIENTS | YIELDS 3–4 CUPS

1 cup iceberg lettuce
2 pints blueberries
1 banana, peeled
½ cup rice milk

1. Place iceberg, blueberries, banana, and half of the rice milk in a blender and blend until thoroughly combined.

2. Add remaining rice milk while blending until desired texture is achieved.

PER 1 CUP SERVING: Calories: 128 | Fat: 1g | Protein: 2g | Sodium: 16mg | Fiber: 5g | Carbohydrates: 32g

Berry Bananas

The deliciously sweet flavors of berries, bananas, and almond milk blend perfectly with the light, crisp romaine to develop a green smoothie that beats any takeout smoothie around.

INGREDIENTS | YIELDS 4–6 CUPS

1 cup romaine lettuce
1 pint blueberries
1 pint raspberries
2 pints strawberries
2 bananas, peeled
1 cup vanilla almond milk
1 cup Greek-style yogurt

1. Place romaine, berries, bananas, and milk in a blender and blend until thoroughly combined.

2. Add Greek-style yogurt while blending until desired texture is achieved.

PER 1 CUP SERVING: Calories: 230 | Fat: 2g | Protein: 9g | Sodium: 66mg | Fiber: 11g | Carbohydrates: 49g

Go Nuts for Chocolate!

Even some of the most dedicated vegans have a soft spot for chocolate. This recipe allows you to create your own thrifty, quick, and easy chocolate smoothies at home while still adhering to the vegan lifestyle.

INGREDIENTS | YIELDS 3–4 CUPS

¼ cup almonds

1 cup vanilla almond milk

2 tablespoons raw powdered cocoa

1 cup watercress

1 banana, peeled

1 tablespoon agave nectar (optional)

1. Combine almonds and ½ cup almond milk in a blender and blend until almonds are completely emulsified.

2. Add cocoa, followed by the watercress, banana, nectar, and remaining ½ cup almond milk while blending until desired texture is achieved.

PER 1 CUP SERVING: Calories: 143 | Fat: 7g | Protein: 4g | Sodium: 56mg | Fiber: 4g | Carbohydrates: 19g

Mango Supreme

Mangoes and bananas make one sweet combination, and with the amazing amounts of vitamins, minerals, and phytochemicals you get from blending them with rich greens, this smoothie is the perfect combination of delightful taste and sound nutrition.

INGREDIENTS | YIELDS 3–4 CUPS

1 cup iceberg lettuce

2 mangoes, peeled and pit removed

1 banana, peeled

2 cups purified water

1. Place iceberg, mangoes, banana, and 1 cup of water in a blender and blend until thoroughly combined.

2. Add remaining cup of water while blending until desired texture is achieved.

PER 1 CUP SERVING: Calories: 96 | Fat: 0g | Protein: 1g | Sodium: 7mg | Fiber: 3g | Carbohydrates: 25g

Just Peachy

Peaches can offer a sweet nectar taste to almost anything . . . even on their own!
Peaches brighten the fresh taste of romaine in this recipe.

INGREDIENTS | YIELDS 3–4 CUPS

1 cup romaine lettuce

3 peaches, pitted (peel removed optional)

1 banana

½ cup water

1. Place romaine, peaches, banana, and ¼ cup of water in a blender and blend until thoroughly combined.

2. Add remaining ¼ cup of water while blending until desired texture is achieved.

PER 1 CUP SERVING: Calories: 72 | Fat: 0g | Protein: 1g | Sodium: 2mg | Fiber: 3g | Carbohydrates: 18g

A Daring Pearing

Because pears aren't in season year round, the frozen option is available
at almost any grocery store and will make equally delicious green smoothies.

INGREDIENTS | YIELDS 3–4 CUPS

1 cup spinach

3 pears, peeled and cored

1 banana, peeled

1 cup purified water

1. Place spinach, pears, banana, and ½ cup water in a blender and blend until thoroughly combined.

2. Add remaining ½ cup water while blending until desired texture is achieved.

PER 1 CUP SERVING: Calories: 105 | Fat: 0g | Protein: 1g | Sodium: 9mg | Fiber: 5g | Carbohydrates: 28g

Great Granny Smith

With a sweet-tart taste that so many people love, Granny Smith apples have even spun off into candy flavors. Try serving this smoothie the next time your kids want sour apple candy.

INGREDIENTS | YIELDS 3–4 CUPS

1 cup spinach

3 Granny Smith apples, peeled and cored

2 bananas

2 cups purified water

1. Place spinach, apples, bananas, and 1 cup of water in a blender and blend until thoroughly combined.

2. Add remaining cup of water while blending until desired texture is achieved.

PER 1 CUP SERVING: Calories: 112 | Fat: 0g | Protein: 1g | Sodium: 9mg | Fiber: 3g | Carbohydrates: 29g

CHAPTER 6

Savory Smoothies

Veggie Variety

With more variety comes a more beneficial array of the important vitamins and nutrients that keep your body running like an efficient machine.

INGREDIENTS | YIELDS 3–4 CUPS

1 cup spinach

1 tomato

1 cucumber, peeled

2 stalks celery

1 garlic clove

1 cup purified water

1. Place spinach, tomato, cucumber, celery, garlic, and ½ cup of purified water in a blender and blend until thoroughly combined.

2. Add remaining ½ cup water while blending until desired texture is achieved.

PER 1 CUP SERVING: Calories: 18 | Fat: 0g | Protein: 1g | Sodium: 26mg | Fiber: 1g | Carbohydrates: 3g

Cucumbers

Cucumbers are available year round. Store them unwashed in your refrigerator for up to ten days. Wash them just before using. Leftover cucumbers can be refrigerated again; just tightly wrap them in plastic and they will keep for up to five days.

A Spicy Assortment

Variety is the spice of life, right? This savory smoothies offers a salty, spicy, and amazingly delicious combination of vegetables.

INGREDIENTS | YIELDS 3–4 CUPS

1 cup arugula

2 carrots, peeled

1 zucchini

1 celery

½ jalapeño, or to taste

1 garlic clove

1 cup purified water

1. Place arugula, carrots, zucchini, celery, jalapeño, garlic, and ½ cup water in a blender and blend until thoroughly combined.

2. Add remaining water while blending until desired texture is achieved.

PER 1 CUP SERVING: Calories: 35 | Fat: 0g | Protein: 2g | Sodium: 49mg | Fiber: 2g | Carbohydrates: 8g

Awesome Asparagus

Rich in vitamins K, A, C, Bs; folate; and a variety of minerals like iron and zinc, this veggie's benefits surpass many others. Introducing 1 cup of asparagus to your daily diet promotes heart health and digestive health and regularity, and it satisfies a daily serving requirement of vegetables.

INGREDIENTS | YIELDS 3–4 CUPS

1 cup romaine lettuce

1 cup asparagus

1 green onion

1 celery stalk

1 garlic clove

2 cups purified water

Juice of ½ lemon

1. Place romaine, asparagus, onion, celery, garlic, and 1 cup of purified water in a blender and blend until thoroughly combined.

2. Add remaining cup of water and lemon juice while blending until desired texture and taste are achieved.

PER 1 CUP SERVING: Calories: 12 | Fat: 0g | Protein: 1g | Sodium: 3mg | Fiber: 1g | Carbohydrates: 3g

Blazing Broccoli

Everybody grew up hearing, "You need to finish your broccoli." It's one veggie that has a bad reputation. The truth is that broccoli is one of the most powerfully packed superfoods you can find!

INGREDIENTS | YIELDS 3–4 CUPS

1 cup spinach

1 cup broccoli

1 carrot, peeled

1 green pepper, cored

½ lime, peeled

2 cups purified water

1. Place spinach, broccoli, carrot, pepper, lime, and 1 cup of purified water in a blender and blend until thoroughly combined.

2. Add remaining 1 cup water while blending until desired texture is achieved.

PER 1 CUP SERVING: Calories: 24 | Fat: 0g | Protein: 1g | Sodium: 27mg | Fiber: 2g | Carbohydrates: 6g

Kale Carrot Combo

Kale is a very strong-tasting green that has many benefits. This recipe pairs it with other strong, and very sweet, vegetables and fruits that blend well with it and make it a delicious addition to any day.

INGREDIENTS | YIELDS 3–4 CUPS

2 kale leaves

4 carrots, peeled

1 apple, cored and peeled

1 banana, peeled

2 cups purified water

1. Place kale leaves, carrots, apple, banana, and 1 cup purified water in a blender and blend until thoroughly combined

2. Add remaining 1 cup of water while blending until desired texture is achieved.

PER 1 CUP SERVING: Calories: 83 | Fat: 0g | Protein: 2g | Sodium: 52mg | Fiber: 4g | Carbohydrates: 21g

Fantastic Fennel

Although it can be found in almost every grocery store's produce section, people rarely purchase or prepare fennel at home. The vitamins and minerals in this veggie make it a must have, and the taste is amazingly unique.

INGREDIENTS | YIELDS 3–4 CUPS

1 cup romaine lettuce

2 fennel bulbs

1 cucumber, peeled

1 carrot, peeled

1 celery stalk

2 cups purified water

1. Place romaine, fennel, cucumber, carrot, celery, and 1 cup of purified water in a blender and blend until thoroughly combined.

2. Add remaining 1 cup of water while blending until desired texture is achieved.

PER 1 CUP SERVING: Calories: 52 | Fat: 0g | Protein: 2g | Sodium: 84mg | Fiber: 5g | Carbohydrates: 12g

Vitamins to the Rescue

Research shows that many antioxidants interact with and protect each other. Vitamin C, for instance, can react with a damaged vitamin E molecule and convert it back to its antioxidant form, while the antioxidant glutathione can return vitamin C to its original form. Studies also show that vitamin C enhances the protective effects of vitamin E.

Spicy Spinach

The taste of spinach can be altered by including it in certain combinations with other strong vegetables and fruits. By using these specific ingredients, especially the cilantro and garlic, this smoothie is one of a kind.

INGREDIENTS | YIELDS 3–4 CUPS

1 cup spinach

1 tomato

1 celery stalk

1–2 tablespoons cilantro

1 garlic clove

2 cups purified water

1. Place spinach, tomato, celery, cilantro, garlic, and 1 cup water in a blender and blend until thoroughly combined.

2. Add remaining 1 cup of water while blending until desired texture is achieved.

PER 1 CUP SERVING: Calories: 13 | Fat: 0g | Protein: 1g | Sodium: 24mg | Fiber: 1g | Carbohydrates: 3g

Garlic

Garlic may be one of the healthiest vegetables you can add to your smoothies. Studies credit it with fighting bladder, skin, colon, and stomach cancer. Eating one to three cloves per day is recommended for optimum results. Placing garlic in your smoothies is an easy way to meet that requirement.

Tangy Tomato

Tomatoes, celery, cilantro, and garlic blend beautifully with arugula in this recipe to deliver a vitamin-rich, tangy smoothie that's absolutely splendid.

INGREDIENTS | YIELDS 3–4 CUPS

1 cup arugula

2 tomatoes

1 celery stalk

2 tablespoons cilantro

1 clove garlic

2 cups purified water

1. Place arugula, tomatoes, celery, cilantro, garlic, and 1 cup purified water in a blender and blend until thoroughly combined.

2. Add remaining 1 cup water while blending until desired texture is achieved.

PER 1 CUP SERVING: Calories: 15 | Fat: 0g | Protein: 1g | Sodium: 15mg | Fiber: 1g | Carbohydrates: 3g

Zippy Zucchini

Zucchini is well known for being a blank canvas in terms of flavor.
Adding savory ingredients with the spicy arugula in this recipe delivers a smoothie with a bite.

INGREDIENTS | YIELDS 3–4 CUPS

1 cup arugula

2 zucchini

1 celery stalk

1 tomato

1 garlic clove

2 cups purified water

1. Place arugula, zucchini, celery, tomato, garlic, and 1 cup water in a blender and blend until thoroughly combined.

2. Add remaining 1 cup of water while blending until desired texture is achieved.

PER 1 CUP SERVING: Calories: 25 | Fat: 0g | Protein: 2g | Sodium: 23mg | Fiber: 2g | Carbohydrates: 5g

Sweet and Savory Beet

Beets and their greens are filled with antioxidants and vitamins. Paired with the flavorful carrots and cucumbers in this smoothie, they create a sweet and delicious smoothie you're sure to enjoy!

INGREDIENTS | YIELDS 3–4 CUPS

1 cup beet greens

2 beets

2 carrots, peeled

1 cucumber, peeled

2 cups purified water

1. Place beet greens, beets, carrots, cucumber, and 1 cup water in a blender and blend until thoroughly combined.

2. Add remaining 1 cup water while blending until desired texture is achieved.

PER 1 CUP SERVING: Calories: 38 | Fat: 0g | Protein: 1g | Sodium: 78mg | Fiber: 3g | Carbohydrates: 8g

Beet Colors

Beets come in many colors, from deep red to orange. They also can be white. The Chioggia beet is called a candy cane beet because it has red and white rings. Small or medium beets are more tender than larger ones. Beets can be enjoyed on their own or flavored with some butter, salt, and pepper for a simple side dish.

Peppers and Onions, Hold the Philly

*The fat-laden Philly cheese steak is a yummy, but nutrient-lacking, meal.
Rather than indulging in a sandwich that leaves you full but running on empty,
try this smoothie that delivers the amazing flavors of onions, peppers, and garlic. Hold the guilt!*

INGREDIENTS | YIELDS 3–4 CUPS

1 cup iceberg lettuce
1 green pepper
1 red pepper
1 green onion
1 clove garlic
2 cups purified water

1. Place iceberg, peppers, onion, garlic, and 1 cup water in a blender and blend until thoroughly combined.

2. Add remaining 1 cup of water while blending until desired texture is achieved.

PER 1 CUP SERVING: Calories: 27 | Fat: 0g | Protein: 1g | Sodium: 8mg | Fiber: 2g | Carbohydrates: 6g

Fantastic Frisée

*Not too many people enjoy flavorful frisée. Take a chance on this delectable green in your smoothie,
and you'll benefit from its richness in vitamins, minerals, antioxidants, and flavor.*

INGREDIENTS | YIELDS 3–4 CUPS

1 cup frisée
1 tomato
1 celery stalk
1 cucumber, peeled
1 garlic clove
2 cups purified water

1. Place frisée, tomato, celery, cucumber, garlic, and 1 cup water in a blender and blend until thoroughly combined.

2. Add remaining 1 cup water while blending until desired texture is achieved.

PER 1 CUP SERVING: Calories: 16 | Fat: 0g | Protein: 1g | Sodium: 16mg | Fiber: 1g | Carbohydrates: 3g

What Makes a Cucumber Bitter?

As a cucumber gets older on the vine, its seeds become larger and more bitter. If you are using an old cucumber, cut it in half and scoop out the seeds with a spoon to eliminate the bitter taste. According to an old wives' tale, the more bitter the vegetable, the better it is for you. But you'll still get the nutritional benefits cucumbers have to offer without the bitter seeds.

The Green Bloody Mary

The alcoholic Bloody Mary may be tempting, but the alcohol can do a load of damage to cells, skin, digestion, and your mind. This green version of the Bloody Mary has all of the necessary ingredients to repair exactly what the alcoholic version destroys!

INGREDIENTS | YIELDS 3–4 CUPS

1 cup watercress

2 tomatoes

2 celery stalks

½ lemon, peeled

1 tablespoon horseradish

½ teaspoon cayenne pepper (optional)

1 cup purified water

1. Place watercress, tomatoes, celery, lemon, horseradish, and cayenne with ½ cup purified water in a blender and blend until thoroughly combined.

2. Add remaining ½ cup water while blending until desired texture is achieved.

PER 1 CUP SERVING: Calories: 19 | Fat: 0g | Protein: 1g | Sodium: 36mg | Fiber: 1g | Carbohydrates: 4g

Cabbage Carrot

Cabbage is one of those important veggies that makes a debut only on special holidays, and then it's usually not prepared or paired in the most nutritious ways. This recipe blends this tasty green with carrots and ginger to deliver a sweet smoothie with a bite!

INGREDIENTS | YIELDS 3–4 CUPS

1 cup green cabbage

3 carrots, peeled

2 celery stalks

1" ginger nodule, peeled and sliced

2 cups purified water

1. Place cabbage, carrots, celery, ginger, and 1 cup water in a blender and blend until thoroughly combined.

2. Add remaining 1 cup water while blending until desired texture is achieved.

PER 1 CUP SERVING: Calories: 30 | Fat: 0g | Protein: 1g | Sodium: 54mg | Fiber: 2g | Carbohydrates: 7g

Powerful Pepper Trio

*The vibrant colors of peppers show their powerful vitamin-rich content,
which makes for a delicious and nutritious treat. This smoothie's mix of spicy arugula,
peppers, and garlic combine for a savory treat you can enjoy anytime.*

INGREDIENTS | YIELDS 3–4 CUPS

1 cup arugula

1 red pepper, cored

1 green pepper, cored

1 yellow pepper, cored

1 garlic clove

2 cups purified water

1. Place arugula, peppers, garlic, and 1 cup of water in a blender and blend until thoroughly combined.

2. Add remaining 1 cup water while blending until desired texture is achieved.

PER 1 CUP SERVING: Calories: 29 | Fat: 0g | Protein: 1g | Sodium: 6mg | Fiber: 2g | Carbohydrates: 7g

The Zesty Zoomer

*Spicy arugula, sweet red pepper, cilantro, and garlic team up
to deliver a spicy and sweet combination in this smoothie.*

INGREDIENTS | YIELDS 3–4 CUPS

1 cup arugula

1 red pepper, cored

2 tablespoons cilantro

1 garlic clove

2 cups purified water

1. Place arugula, pepper, cilantro, garlic, and 1 cup water in a blender and blend until thoroughly combined.

2. Add remaining 1 cup water, if needed, while blending until desired texture is achieved.

PER 1 CUP SERVING: Calories: 16 | Fat: 0g | Protein: 1g | Sodium: 7mg | Fiber: 1g | Carbohydrates: 3g

Great Garlic

Although it may keep vampires away, this strong addition can do even more for your health.
Just one small clove of garlic helps promote a strong heart,
and makes almost anything taste absolutely delightful.

INGREDIENTS | YIELDS 3–4 CUPS

1 cup spinach

1 celery stalk

1 tomato

3 garlic cloves

2 cups purified water

1. Place spinach, celery, tomato, garlic, and 1 cup water in a blender and blend until thoroughly combined.

2. Add remaining 1 cup water, if needed, while blending until desired texture is achieved.

PER 1 CUP SERVING: Calories: 12 | Fat: 0g | Protein: 1g | Sodium: 18mg | Fiber: 1g | Carbohydrates: 3g

A Savory Celery Celebration

Celery is a powerful ingredient in any diet needing lower sodium and more water retention.
Pills and powders barely hold water in comparison to this delightfully fresh veggie.

INGREDIENTS | YIELDS 3–4 CUPS

1 cup watercress

3 celery stalks

1 cucumber, peeled

1 garlic clove

1 cup purified water

1. Place watercress, celery, cucumber, garlic, and ½ cup water in a blender and blend until thoroughly combined.

2. Add remaining ½ cup water while blending until desired texture is achieved.

PER 1 CUP SERVING: Calories: 13 | Fat: 0g | Protein: 1g | Sodium: 30mg | Fiber: 1g | Carbohydrates: 2g

Savory Squash Surprise

When you take a look at the color of this smoothie, you'll see the vibrant colors of the veggies, and thus their valuable nutrition. The bright-green spinach, yellow squash, and orange carrot combine for an aesthetically and palate-pleasing smoothie.

INGREDIENTS | YIELDS 3–4 CUPS

1 cup spinach

½ butternut squash, peeled, deseeded, and cubed

1 carrot, peeled

2 garlic cloves

2 cups purified water

1. Place spinach, squash, carrot, garlic, and 1 cup of water in a blender and blend until thoroughly combined.

2. Add remaining 1 cup of water while blending until desired texture is achieved.

PER 1 CUP SERVING: Calories: 18 | Fat: 0g | Protein: 1g | Sodium: 20mg | Fiber: 1g | Carbohydrates: 4g

The Temptation of Turnips

*When was the last time you ate a turnip? Rich in nutrition,
this rarely enjoyed root vegetable is a great addition to any diet.*

INGREDIENTS | YIELDS 3–4 CUPS

1 cup romaine lettuce

2 turnips, peeled and cut best for blender's ability

2 carrots, peeled

2 celery stalks

2 cups purified water

1. Place romaine, turnips, carrots, celery, and 1 cup water in a blender and blend until thoroughly combined.

2. Add remaining 1 cup of water while blending until desired texture is achieved.

PER 1 CUP SERVING: Calories: 35 | Fat: 0g | Protein: 1g | Sodium: 81mg | Fiber: 3g | Carbohydrates: 8g

Turnip Lanterns

Pumpkins aren't the only vegetable that have been carved for Halloween. The Irish started the tradition of carving lanterns on Halloween, but originally turnips were used. Turnip lanterns were left on doorsteps in order to ward off evil spirits.

Turnip lanterns are an old tradition; since inaugural Halloween festivals in Ireland and Scotland, turnips (rutabaga) have been carved out and used as candle lanterns. At Samhain, candle lanterns carved from turnips—Samhnag—were part of the traditional Celtic festival. Large turnips were hollowed out, carved with faces, and placed in windows to ward off harmful spirits.

CHAPTER 7

Vegan Smoothies

Mango Berry

Watercress acts as a beautiful background green for this deliciously sweet and smooth recipe. The mangoes, raspberries, and coconut milk provide a healthy serving of vitamins, minerals, and strong antioxidants.

INGREDIENTS | YIELDS 3–4 CUPS

1 cup watercress

2 mangoes, pitted and peeled

2 pints raspberries

1½ cups coconut milk

Mangoes and Digestion

When starting out a new raw-food diet, some people report having difficulty digesting the amount and type of fiber found in the healthy ingredients like greens and fresh fruits. Mangoes aid in digestion by combating acidity and uncomfortable acids in the digestive system and create a more placid, balanced system capable of a smooth, regular digestive process.

1. Place watercress, mangoes, raspberries, and half of the coconut milk in a blender and blend until thoroughly combined.

2. Add remaining coconut milk while blending until desired texture is achieved.

PER 1 CUP SERVING: Calories: 316 | Fat: 19g | Protein: 4g | Sodium: 18mg | Fiber: 12g | Carbohydrates: 39g

Delicious Bananas and Berries

While satisfying your sweet tooth with this delicious blend of bananas, blueberries, and strawberries, consider boosting your daily protein intake by adding a scoop of whey protein or soy protein powder to the mix.

INGREDIENTS | YIELDS 3–4 CUPS

1 cup romaine lettuce

2 bananas, peeled

1 pint strawberries

1 pint blueberries

2 cups almond milk

Soy Versus Whey

For the devout vegan who consumes absolutely no animal products, including dairy or eggs, soy protein is the way to go. Soy protein has absolutely no milk derivatives in its makeup and is acceptable for a strict dairy-free diet. For vegetarians who welcome dairy additions in their diet, whey is acceptable as well as soy. Whey is made from milk byproducts, making it suitable for those who include dairy in their diet.

1. Place romaine, bananas, berries, and 1 cup almond milk in a blender and blend until thoroughly combined.

2. Add remaining 1 cup of almond milk while blending until desired texture is achieved.

PER 1 CUP SERVING: Calories: 316 | Fat: 19g | Protein: 4g | Sodium: 18mg | Fiber: 12g | Carbohydrates: 39g

Peachy Orange Banana

Delightfully refreshing citrus paired with sweet peaches and smooth bananas make this smoothie a delicious treat for breakfast, lunch, a snack, or dessert.

INGREDIENTS | YIELDS 3–4 CUPS

1 cup watercress

1 orange, peeled

2 peaches, pitted

1 banana, peeled

1 cup coconut milk

1. Place watercress, orange, peaches, banana, and ½ cup coconut milk in a blender and blend until thoroughly combined.

2. Add remaining ½ cup coconut milk while blending until desired texture is achieved.

PER 1 CUP SERVING: Calories: 183 | Fat: 12g | Protein: 3g | Sodium: 11mg | Fiber: 3g | Carbohydrates: 20g

Ahhh, Sweet Greens!

Apples and spinach in the same smoothie may seem like an unlikely pair, but one sip of this blend will have even the harshest skeptic agreeing that the duo makes a delicious treat.

INGREDIENTS | YIELDS 3–4 CUPS

1 cup spinach

2 bananas, peeled

2 apples, cored and peeled

2 cups almond milk

Fiber Benefits

Leafy greens, vegetables, and fruits all contain some amount of this miracle substance. Because fiber is almost completely unable to be digested by the human body, we benefit from its tendency to require more chewing time, make our stomachs feel full, and clear our intestinal tracts by remaining nearly intact throughout digestion. Although fiber is available in pill and powder forms, they are a far cry from a healthy bowl of spinach, broccoli, or fresh fruit.

1. Place spinach, bananas, apples, and 1 cup almond milk in a blender and blend until thoroughly combined.

2. Add remaining 1 cup of almond milk while blending until desired texture is achieved.

PER 1 CUP SERVING: Calories: 147 | Fat: 2g | Protein: 2g | Sodium: 82mg | Fiber: 4g | Carbohydrates: 34g

Green Citrus

Vitamin C and a wide variety of other vitamins, minerals, fiber, antioxidants, and amazing flavor in this smoothie create a delicious way to combat illnesses in the tastiest way possible!

INGREDIENTS | YIELDS 3–4 CUPS

1 cup watercress

1 grapefruit, peeled

2 oranges, peeled

1 banana, peeled

1 cup purified water

1. Place watercress, grapefruit, oranges, banana, and ½ cup water in a blender and blend until thoroughly combined.

2. Add remaining ½ cup water while blending until desired texture is achieved.

PER 1 CUP SERVING: Calories: 90 | Fat: 0g | Protein: 2g | Sodium: 5mg | Fiber: 4g | Carbohydrates: 23g

Flowery Fruits

Although these fruits don't flower, dandelion greens do make a pretty addition to this wonderful smoothie. The dandelion greens, arugula, and pineapple create a splendidly sweet combination.

INGREDIENTS | YIELDS 3–4 CUPS

½ cup dandelion greens

½ cup arugula

2 cups pineapple, peeled and cored

1 banana, peeled

2 cups coconut milk

1. Place dandelion greens, arugula, pineapple, banana, and 1 cup coconut milk in a blender and blend until thoroughly combined.

2. Add remaining 1 cup of coconut milk while blending until desired texture is achieved.

PER 1 CUP SERVING: Calories: 290 | Fat: 24g | Protein: 3g | Sodium: 22mg | Fiber: 1g | Carbohydrates: 20g

The Rich Flavors of Protein

You can easily add protein powders to your green smoothies. No longer bland or chalky, protein powders are available in a wide variety of flavors and flavor combinations that will provide a healthy helping of protein while satisfying your sweet tooth. Chocolate, banana cream, and many more flavors are now available. Blend them into these recipes to increase your daily protein intake while adhering to your vegan diet.

Apple Peach

Apples, peaches, and almond milk create a sweet, smooth blend that complements the green watercress. If you're looking for a healthy snack, skip the processed sweets and energy drinks and opt for this quick and easy blend that will give you sustainable energy for the rest of your day.

INGREDIENTS | YIELDS 3–4 CUPS

1 cup watercress

3 peaches, pitted

2 apples, cored and peeled

2 cups almond milk

1. Place watercress, peaches, apples, and 1 cup almond milk in a blender and blend until thoroughly combined.

2. Add remaining 1 cup almond milk while blending until desired texture is achieved.

PER 1 CUP SERVING: Calories: 137 | Fat: 2g | Protein: 2g | Sodium: 79mg | Fiber: 4g | Carbohydrates: 32g

Ginger Apple

The fiber from the romaine and apples offers the benefit of an optimal digestive system, and the ginger soothes any stomach discomfort. This recipe is highly recommended for those days you may feel especially irregular or uncomfortable.

INGREDIENTS | YIELDS 3–4 CUPS

1 cup romaine lettuce

3 apples, cored and peeled

1 tablespoon ginger, peeled

2 cups almond milk

1. Place romaine, apples, ginger, and 1 cup almond milk in a blender and blend until thoroughly combined.

2. Add remaining 1 cup almond milk while blending until desired texture is achieved.

PER 1 CUP SERVING: Calories: 119 | Fat: 2g | Protein: 1g | Sodium: 78mg | Fiber: 4g | Carbohydrates: 28g

Fiber and Ginger Combination

Ginger is hailed as one of nature's most potent medicinal plants, with its most well-known cure being for stomach ailments. Combining ginger with the fiber found in fruits and leafy greens is an effective way to clean out the digestive tract, promote the release of good digestive enzymes, and soothe the stomach.

Very Cherry Pears

If you like cherry, vanilla, and pears, this recipe is for you!
Add a scoop of soy protein powder to make the health benefits of this smoothie even greater.

INGREDIENTS | YIELDS 3–4 CUPS

1 cup iceberg lettuce

2 pears, cored

1 banana, peeled

1 cup cherries, pitted

½ vanilla bean pulp

2 cups almond milk

1. Place iceberg, pears, banana, cherries, vanilla bean pulp, and 1 cup almond milk in a blender and blend until thoroughly combined.

2. Add remaining 1 cup almond milk while blending until desired texture is achieved.

PER 1 CUP SERVING: Calories: 150 | Fat: 2g | Protein: 2g | Sodium: 78mg | Fiber: 5g | Carbohydrates: 35g

Go, Cocoa!

Bursting with flavor, this smoothie provides more nutrition than you would think.
Vitamins, minerals, and antioxidants beam from each ingredient!

INGREDIENTS | YIELDS 3–4 CUPS

1 cup romaine lettuce

2 bananas, peeled

1 tablespoon raw cocoa powder

½ vanilla bean pulp

2 cups almond milk

Fight Cancer with Cocoa

With almost every candy bar available consisting of milk products, devout vegans are left to purchase hard-to-find vegan candy, or create their own desserts at home. With the purchase of raw carob or cocoa powder, your kitchen can be turned into a chocolate shop of homemade delectable delights! Providing strong cancer-fighting antioxidants, these raw forms of chocolate bliss can extend your life while satisfying your sweet tooth.

1. Place romaine, bananas, cocoa powder, vanilla bean pulp, and 1 cup almond milk in a blender and blend until thoroughly combined.

2. Add remaining 1 cup of almond milk while blending until desired texture is achieved.

PER 1 CUP SERVING: Calories: 102 | Fat: 2g | Protein: 2g | Sodium: 77mg | Fiber: 3g | Carbohydrates: 23g

Citrus Berry

Blend these delightfully fresh fruits with the refreshing taste of watercress, and the only overwhelming feeling you'll encounter is pure pleasure. Your mouth, mind, and body will all benefit from the vitamins and minerals.

INGREDIENTS | YIELDS 3–4 CUPS

1 cup watercress

2 oranges, peeled

1 cup strawberries

1 cup blueberries

1 cup coconut milk

1. Place watercress, oranges, strawberries, blueberries, and ½ cup coconut milk in a blender and blend until thoroughly combined.

2. Add remaining ½ cup coconut milk while blending until desired texture is achieved.

PER 1 CUP SERVING: Calories: 188 | Fat: 12g | Protein: 3g | Sodium: 12mg | Fiber: 4g | Carbohydrates: 21g

Pears with a Tart Twist

Providing an amazing percentage of essential vitamins and minerals needed for the optimal functioning of your mind and body, this smoothie is a sweet, tart, and smart way to pep up your day!

INGREDIENTS | YIELDS 4–6 CUPS

4 cups romaine lettuce

4 pears, cored

1 banana, peeled

6 tablespoons lemon juice

2 cups purified water

1. Place romaine, pears, banana, lemon juice, and 1 cup water in a blender and blend until thoroughly combined.

2. Add remaining 1 cup of water while blending until desired texture is achieved.

PER 1 CUP SERVING: Calories: 94 | Fat: 0g | Protein: 1g | Sodium: 6mg | Fiber: 5g | Carbohydrates: 25g

Amazing Avocados

*If you're looking to add the good fats that can be found in nuts, seeds,
and certain fruits to your diet, avocados should definitely be in your kitchen.
The creamy texture of avocados makes a perfect addition to salads, soups, and smoothies.*

INGREDIENTS | YIELDS 3–4 CUPS

1 cup spinach

2 avocados, peeled and seeds removed

1 lime, peeled

1 cup purified water

1 cup vegan Greek-style yogurt

Avocados and Oral Cancer

Although avocados have been found to fight the cancer-causing free radicals of colon, breast, and prostate cancers, the most notable protective benefit avocados create in the human body is the protection against oral cancer. With a 50 percent mortality rate most commonly due to late detection, oral cancer is a preventative cancer that can be helped with the addition of just 2 ounces of avocado to your diet.

1. Place spinach, avocados, lime, ½ cup water, and ½ cup yogurt in a blender and blend until thoroughly combined.

2. Add remaining ½ cup water and ½ cup yogurt while blending until desired texture is achieved.

PER 1 CUP SERVING: Calories: 200 | Fat: 15g | Protein: 8g | Sodium: 38mg | Fiber: 7g | Carbohydrates: 13g

Guacamole, Anyone?

This vibrant smoothie includes all of the wonderful ingredients of the much-loved, extremely healthy snack.

INGREDIENTS | YIELDS 3–4 CUPS

1 cup watercress

1 avocado, peeled and seed removed

1 lime, peeled

1 tomato

1 green onion

1 celery stalk

¼ cup cilantro

1 cup purified water

1. Place watercress, avocado, lime, tomato, onion, celery, cilantro, and ½ cup water in a blender and blend until thoroughly combined.

2. Add remaining ½ cup water while blending until desired texture is achieved.

PER 1 CUP SERVING: Calories: 95 | Fat: 7g | Protein: 2g | Sodium: 19mg | Fiber: 5g | Carbohydrates: 8g

Flaxseed in Your Smoothie

Although most of the protein powders available are sweet flavors, you can find plain ones that will add protein without altering the taste. A different type of health-benefiting addition is ground flaxseed. Rich in omega-3s, powerful in fighting cancers, and well known for regulating blood pressure, these slightly nutty-tasting seeds boost your green smoothie to a super green smoothie!

Broccoli Carrot

*Broccoli is not only a vitamin- and mineral-packed green veggie,
it also contains more protein than most other veggie options. Vegans and vegetarians
can find a good source of extra protein in this vibrant green vegetable.*

INGREDIENTS | YIELDS 3–4 CUPS

1 cup romaine lettuce

1 cup broccoli

2 carrots, peeled

2 cups purified water

1. Place romaine, broccoli, carrots, and 1 cup of water in a blender and blend until thoroughly combined.

2. Add remaining 1 cup of water while blending until desired texture is achieved.

PER 1 CUP SERVING: Calories: 22 | Fat: 0g | Protein: 1g | Sodium: 32mg | Fiber: 2g | Carbohydrates: 5g

Zucchini Apple

Many people heavily season zucchini when preparing it as a side dish due to it's somewhat bland taste. In this recipe, no seasonings are needed! The sweet carrots and apples blend beautifully with the spinach and zucchini to deliver maximum flavor.

INGREDIENTS | YIELDS 3–4 CUPS

1 cup spinach

1 zucchini

3 carrots, peeled

2 red apples, cored and peeled

2 cups purified water

Benefits of Raw Zucchini

Raw food enthusiasts embrace the idea of consuming minimally cooked foods because heat (above 115°F) drastically reduces the vitamins, minerals, phytochemicals, and antioxidants found in fruits and vegetables. Zucchini is usually sautéed, baked, or roasted with salt and seasonings to add flavor. By blending this healthy veggie in your smoothie, you'll benefit from it in its pure form, without destructive heat and counterproductive seasonings.

1. Place spinach, zucchini, carrots, apples, and 1 cup water in a blender and blend until thoroughly combined.

2. Add remaining 1 cup of water while blending until desired texture is achieved.

PER 1 CUP SERVING: Calories: 76 | Fat: 0g | Protein: 1g | Sodium: 46mg | Fiber: 4g | Carbohydrates: 19g

Red and Green Smoothie

The ingredients in this recipe offer a wide variety of health benefits.
Iron, powerful vitamin C, fiber, antioxidants, and natural diuretics combine
to make this a beneficial treat that packs plenty of flavor.

INGREDIENTS | YIELDS 3–4 CUPS

1 cup spinach

1 cucumber, peeled

2 celery stalks

2 red Gala apples, cored and peeled

1 lemon, peeled

1 lime, peeled

1 cup purified water

1. Place spinach, cucumber, celery, apples, lemon, lime, and ½ cup water in a blender and blend until thoroughly combined.

2. Add additional ½ cup water, if needed, while blending until desired texture is achieved.

PER 1 CUP SERVING: Calories: 68 | Fat: 0g | Protein: 1g | Sodium: 25mg | Fiber: 4g | Carbohydrates: 18g

Sweet Asparagus

The sweet tang of oranges and lemons blend with the unique taste
of asparagus and watercress to give this smoothie a wide variety of taste sensations.

INGREDIENTS | YIELDS 3–4 CUPS

1 cup watercress

1 cup asparagus

1 lemon, peeled

1 orange, peeled

1 cup purified water

1. Place watercress, asparagus, lemon, orange, and ½ cup water in a blender and blend until thoroughly combined.

2. Add remaining ½ cup water while blending until desired texture is achieved.

PER 1 CUP SERVING: Calories: 33 | Fat: 0g | Protein: 2g | Sodium: 6mg | Fiber: 2g | Carbohydrates: 8g

Beany Spinach

One of the most common bean dishes people enjoy is chili. The high sodium content and heat provide minimum health benefits found in fiber- and protein-packed beans. This smoothie maximizes the benefits by keeping them in the raw form.

INGREDIENTS | YIELDS 3–4 CUPS

1 cup spinach

1 cup red kidney beans, soaked and drained

1 cup northern white beans, soaked and drained

½ teaspoon cayenne

2 cups purified water

1. Place spinach, kidney beans, white beans, and cayenne pepper with 1 cup water in a blender and blend until thoroughly combined.

2. Add remaining 1 cup of water while blending until desired texture is achieved.

PER 1 CUP SERVING: Calories: 311 | Fat: 1g | Protein: 21g | Sodium: 26mg | Fiber: 21g | Carbohydrates: 57g

Cayenne for Digestive Health

You would think that such a spicy addition would cause stomach discomfort, but this pepper has amazing benefits. Cayenne has the ability to promote a digestive enzyme that works to kill bad bacteria ingested from foods while also promoting the good bacteria that optimizes the digestive process. As if that wasn't enough, these hot little items also work so hard to fight off bad bacteria, they actually prevent stomach ulcers!

An Orange Broccoli Blend

*Thanks to the fiber, vitamins, and minerals in each of these ingredients,
this smoothie is tasty and hearty enough to replace any meal.*

INGREDIENTS | YIELDS 3–4 CUPS

1 cup romaine lettuce

1 cup broccoli

1 zucchini

2 carrots, peeled

2 cups purified water

1. Place romaine, broccoli, zucchini, carrots, and 1 cup of water in a blender and blend until thoroughly combined.

2. Add remaining 1 cup of water while blending until desired texture is achieved.

PER 1 CUP SERVING: Calories: 30 | Fat: 0g | Protein: 2g | Sodium: 37mg | Fiber: 2g | Carbohydrates: 6g

Carrot Asparagus

*This blend is yet another recipe that can easily have its vitamin
and mineral content improved with the addition of ground flaxseeds.
The addition of flax in this smoothie would lend a delicious hint of nutty flavor.*

INGREDIENTS | YIELDS 3–4 CUPS

1 cup watercress
1 cup asparagus
2 carrots, peeled
2 cups water

Flaxseeds

Flaxseed is a common product found in almost every grocery store. Available organic, nonorganic, ground, and whole, flaxseeds can be found in aisles with nuts or near produce. You can purchase the whole-seed product and use them in sandwiches, salads, and main dishes by using a coffee grinder and grinding them until thoroughly powdered. If the thought of grinding your own flaxseeds sounds intimidating or time consuming, the ground product may be a wiser option.

1. Place watercress, asparagus, carrots, and 1 cup water in a blender and blend until thoroughly combined.

2. Add remaining 1 cup of water while blending until desired texture is achieved.

PER 1 CUP SERVING: Calories: 20 | Fat: 0g | Protein: 1g | Sodium: 28mg | Fiber: 2g | Carbohydrates: 4g

Green Sweet Citrus

This recipe is a wonderfully refreshing option for any time your body and mind may need a boost. The mildly peppery taste of watercress combines with the citrus flavors to develop a light and refreshing vitamin-packed treat.

INGREDIENTS | YIELDS 3–4 CUPS

1 cup watercress
1 grapefruit, peeled
2 oranges, peeled
½" ginger, peeled
½ lemon, peeled
1 cup purified water

1. Place watercress, grapefruit, oranges, ginger, lemon, and ½ cup water in a blender and blend until thoroughly combined.

2. Add remaining ½ cup water while blending until desired texture is achieved.

PER 1 CUP SERVING: Calories: 67 | Fat: 0g | Protein: 2g | Sodium: 5mg | Fiber: 3g | Carbohydrates: 17g

Veggie Delight

If you're in the mood for a refreshingly savory smoothie, this one might be just what you're looking for! The ingredients create a splendid smoothie that may be delicious and filling enough to take the place of dinner.

INGREDIENTS | YIELDS 4–6 CUPS

1 cup romaine lettuce
2 tomatoes
1 zucchini
2 celery stalks
1 cucumber
½ cup green onions
2 garlic cloves
2 cups purified water

1. Place romaine, tomatoes, zucchini, celery, cucumber, green onions, garlic, and 1 cup water in a blender and blend until thoroughly combined.

2. Add remaining 1 cup of water, if needed, while blending until desired texture is achieved.

PER 1 CUP SERVING: Calories: 28 | Fat: 0g | Protein: 1g | Sodium: 6mg | Fiber: 1g | Carbohydrates: 6g

CHAPTER 8

Smoothies for Cleansing and Detox Diets

Cleansing Cranberry

If you're looking for a sweet and tangy treat, urinary tract infection relief, or both,
this smoothie is for you. The combination of cranberries, cucumber, lemon,
and ginger give this smoothie the power to cleanse your body while delivering a taste sensation.

INGREDIENTS | YIELDS 4–6 CUPS

1 cup watercress

2 pints cranberries

2 cucumbers, peeled

½ lemon, peeled

½" ginger, peeled

2 cups purified water

1. Place watercress, cranberries, cucumbers, lemon, ginger, and 1 cup of purified water in a blender and blend until thoroughly combined.

2. Add the remaining 1 cup of water while blending, as needed, until desired texture is achieved.

PER 1 CUP SERVING: Calories: 41 | Fat: 0g | Protein: 1g | Sodium: 7mg | Fiber: 4g | Carbohydrates: 10g

The Cleansing Power of Cranberries

Cranberries are packed with strong antioxidants and an abundance of vitamins, minerals, and phytochemicals. Not only do these bright-red berries promote health in almost every area of the body, they do wonders for cleansing bad bacteria out of the urinary tract while promoting an inviting environment for bladder health. Most store-bought cranberry juices contain mixtures of sugars and other juices.

Cucumber Zing

*Cucumbers offer a wide variety of important vitamins and minerals while lending
a refreshing and hydrating background to the spicy ginger in this smoothie.
This blend will whet your appetite while cleansing your body and building your immunity!*

INGREDIENTS | YIELDS 3–4 CUPS

1 cup watercress

2 cucumbers, peeled

2 oranges, peeled

¼" ginger, peeled

1 cup purified water

1. Place watercress, cucumbers, oranges, ginger, and ½ cup water in a blender and blend until thoroughly combined.

2. Add remaining ½ cup water while blending, as needed, until desired texture is achieved.

PER 1 CUP SERVING: Calories: 57 | Fat: 0g | Protein: 2g | Sodium: 7mg | Fiber: 3g | Carbohydrates: 13g

Papaya Berry Blend

This recipe combines the crispness of romaine with the sweet flavors of papaya and strawberries to make an enjoyable blend that flushes toxins while promoting optimal health.

INGREDIENTS | YIELDS 3–4 CUPS

1 cup romaine lettuce

2 papayas, seeds removed

1 cup strawberries

1 cup purified water

Eat Papaya for Overall Health

When sweetening your smoothie with papaya, it's important to note that this fruit provides an abundance of vitamins C and A. Together, these vitamins promote healthy cell growth and repair while improving the body's ability to fight off illness and disease. With the goal of detoxifying your body, fruits that provide a great source of these vitamins are a must have in your daily diet. Papayas are a one-stop shop for both!

1. Place romaine, papayas, strawberries, and ½ cup purified water in a blender and blend until thoroughly combined.

2. Add remaining ½ cup of water while blending, as needed, until desired texture is achieved.

PER 1 CUP SERVING: Calories: 73 | Fat: 0g | Protein: 1g | Sodium: 7mg | Fiber: 4g | Carbohydrates: 18g

The Bright Bloat Beater

With important vitamins and minerals from the watercress, antioxidants from the blueberries, potassium from the bananas, and vitamin C from the lemon, this smoothie is powerful in fighting free radicals and promoting overall health.

INGREDIENTS | YIELDS 3–4 CUPS

1 cup watercress
2 cups blueberries
2 bananas, peeled
½ lemon, peeled
2 cups purified water

1. Place watercress, blueberries, bananas, lemon, and 1 cup of water in a blender and blend until thoroughly combined.

2. Add remaining 1 cup of water while blending, as needed, until desired texture is achieved.

PER 1 CUP SERVING: Calories: 98 | Fat: 0g | Protein: 1g | Sodium: 7mg | Fiber: 4g | Carbohydrates: 25g

Ginger and Apple Cleansing Blend

*With loads of fiber from the spinach and apples, ginger makes
a star-studded appearance as a lightly spicy and aromatic addition in this recipe.
It will keep your detox on track with a delightfully sweet twist.*

INGREDIENTS | YIELDS 3–4 CUPS

1 cup spinach

3 apples, peeled and cored

½" ginger, peeled

2 cups purified water

The Importance of Fiber in Cleansing

Apples are sometimes referred to as "nature's scrub brushes" because of the powerful amount of fiber they contain. Found in deep greens, vegetables, and fruits, fiber plays an important role in helping your body rid itself of waste products that may be causing irregularity. The indigestible fibers that pass through the digestive system literally sweep lingering waste with them as they leave the body. In the process of cleansing your body, moving the waste out is an important factor.

1. Place spinach, apples, ginger, and 1 cup of water in a blender and blend until thoroughly combined.

2. Add remaining 1 cup of water while blending, as needed, until desired texture is achieved.

PER 1 CUP SERVING: Calories: 60 | Fat: 0g | Protein: 1g | Sodium: 8mg | Fiber: 2g | Carbohydrates: 16g

Alcohol Recovery Recipe

*Although this smoothie may not relieve that pounding headache,
it will definitely assist your liver in flushing out the toxins provided by alcohol consumption.
This delightful blend will get your body back on track!*

INGREDIENTS | YIELDS 3–4 CUPS

1 cup spinach

3 carrots, peeled

2 apples, peeled and cored

1 beet

2½ cups purified water

Combating the Effects of Alcohol

Because alcohol can really do a number on your liver, it is important to supply your body with the best foods to maintain your liver's optimal functioning following heavy alcohol consumption. Spinach, carrots, apples, beets, lemon, wheatgrass, and grapefruit have shown to be true super-foods when it comes to purging the liver of harmful toxins. In addition, they are also high in vitamin C and promote health while minimizing feelings of moodiness and depression.

1. Place spinach, carrots, apples, beet, and half of the water in a blender and blend until thoroughly combined.

2. Add remaining half of the water while blending, as needed, until desired texture is achieved.

PER 1 CUP SERVING: Calories: 68 | Fat: 0g | Protein: 1g | Sodium: 56mg | Fiber: 3g | Carbohydrates: 17g

Broccoli for Bladder Health

Broccoli can aid in promoting bladder health with an abundance of vitamins, minerals, and phytochemicals that far exceeds those contained in other fruits and veggies.

INGREDIENTS | YIELDS 3–4 CUPS

1 cup watercress

1 cup broccoli spears

3 red Gala apples, peeled and cored

2 cups purified water

The Important Vitamins and Minerals in Broccoli

Broccoli probably isn't the superfood that comes to mind when you think of cleansing, but this super veggie provides far more vitamins and nutrients than you would think. A single serving of broccoli includes the important vitamins A, B, C, and K along with fiber, zinc, folic acid, magnesium, iron, and beta-carotene.

1. Place watercress, broccoli, apples, and 1 cup water in a blender and blend until thoroughly combined.

2. Add remaining 1 cup of water while blending, as needed, until desired texture is achieved.

PER 1 CUP SERVING: Calories: 67 | Fat: 0g | Protein: 1g | Sodium: 13mg | Fiber: 2g | Carbohydrates: 17g

The Spicy Savior

The ginger in this recipe is what gives this smoothie the spicy zing!
The watercress, carrots, broccoli, and ginger all combine for a filling meal replacement in any detox diet.

INGREDIENTS | YIELDS 3–4 CUPS

1 cup watercress

1 cup broccoli spears

3 carrots, peeled

½" ginger, peeled

2 cups purified water

1. Place watercress, broccoli, carrots, ginger, and 1 cup of water in a blender and blend until thoroughly combined.

2. Add remaining 1 cup of water while blending, as needed, until desired texture is achieved.

PER 1 CUP SERVING: Calories: 28 | Fat: 0g | Protein: 1g | Sodium: 45mg | Fiber: 2g | Carbohydrates: 6g

Sweet and Spicy Spinach

Combining spinach with deliciously sweet apples and bananas and slightly spicy ginger can make even the most devout spinach skeptic enjoy this nutritious rich-green veggie as a part of a detox diet.

INGREDIENTS | YIELDS 3–4 CUPS

1 cup spinach

3 apples, cored and peeled

2 bananas, peeled

½ lemon, peeled

2 cups purified water

1. Place spinach, apples, bananas, lemon, and 1 cup purified water in a blender and blend until thoroughly combined.

2. Add remaining 1 cup purified water while blending, as needed, until desired texture is achieved.

PER 1 CUP SERVING: Calories: 114 | Fat: 0g | Protein: 1g | Sodium: 9mg | Fiber: 3g | Carbohydrates: 30g

Berries for Bladder Health

Combining rich berries with super fruits and veggies in this recipe gives your bladder a variety of important vitamins and nutrients that will promote bladder detoxification and health!

INGREDIENTS | YIELDS 3–4 CUPS

1 cup romaine lettuce

2 cups blueberries

1 cup cranberries

1 apple, cored and peeled

1 banana, peeled

½" ginger, peeled

2 cups purified water

1. Place romaine, berries, apple, banana, ginger, and 1 cup water in a blender and blend until thoroughly combined.

2. Add remaining 1 cup of water while blending, as needed, until desired texture is achieved.

PER 1 CUP SERVING: Calories: 102 | Fat: 0g | Protein: 1g | Sodium: 5mg | Fiber: 4g | Carbohydrates: 26g

Berries Aren't Just for UTIs

Well-known for promoting urinary tract health, the antioxidant-rich berries in this recipe also promote a healthy bladder environment. Combining a variety of these rich berries only compounds their benefits. The berries help alleviate symptoms associated with bladder and urinary tract issues, including minimizing discomfort associated with frequent urination, bladder infections, and urinary tract infections.

Carrot Cleanser

This simple recipe takes little time to make and tastes absolutely delicious!
The carrots and lemon do a complementary balancing act that provides a sweet and tangy twist.

INGREDIENTS | YIELDS 3–4 CUPS

1 cup spinach

4 carrots, peeled and tops removed

1 lemon, peeled

2 cups purified water

Carrots as Superfoods

Harnessing the powerful vitamins and minerals contained in carrots while you're on a detoxifying cleanse can help in many ways. The beta-carotene that gives carrots their vibrant color is not only important for eye health but is also a strong cancer-fighting antioxidant that protects cells against harmful free radicals and promotes optimal cell functioning. Carrots also lower the risk of heart disease, cancers, and type 2 diabetes and provide sound nutrition for pregnancy and night vision.

1. Place spinach, carrots, lemon, and 1 cup of water in a blender and blend until thoroughly combined.

2. Add remaining 1 cup of water while blending, as needed, until desired texture is achieved.

PER 1 CUP SERVING: Calories: 31 | Fat: 0g | Protein: 1g | Sodium: 51mg | Fiber: 2g | Carbohydrates: 7g

Green Garlic

This savory delight is sure to cleanse your senses. Garlic is the small ingredient that makes a big impact. Not only does the flavor blend nicely with the other ingredients, it provides liver-cleansing health benefits.

INGREDIENTS | YIELDS 3–4 CUPS

1 cup spinach

1 zucchini, skin intact

¼ cup parsley

2–3 cloves garlic, depending upon size

2 cups purified water

1. Place the spinach, zucchini, parsley, garlic, and 1 cup of water in a blender and blend until thoroughly combined.

2. Add remaining 1 cup of water while blending, as needed, until desired texture is achieved.

PER 1 CUP SERVING: Calories: 13 | Fat: 0g | Protein: 1g | Sodium: 16mg | Fiber: 1g | Carbohydrates: 3g

Fabulous Fiber Flush

*Kale provides an abundance of vitamins A and K.
Combined with the iron- and folate-rich broccoli, pectin-providing apples,
and beta-carotene-filled carrot, the kale makes this smoothie a completely fiber-filled one.*

INGREDIENTS | YIELDS 3–4 CUPS

2 large kale leaves

1 cup broccoli

2 apples, peeled and cored

1 carrot, peeled

½ lemon, peeled

2 cups purified water

1. Place kale, broccoli, apples, carrot, lemon, and 1 cup of water in a blender and blend until thoroughly combined.

2. Add remaining 1 cup of water while blending, as needed, until desired texture is achieved.

PER 1 CUP SERVING: Calories: 71 | Fat: 0g | Protein: 2g | Sodium: 35mg | Fiber: 3g | Carbohydrates: 17g

Colorful Cleansing Combo

*This colorful combination of vegetables makes a visually
and palate-pleasing creation. The ingredients provide a wealth of vitamins
and minerals that will cleanse while optimizing digestive health and comfort.*

INGREDIENTS | YIELDS 3–4 CUPS

1 cup watercress

3 carrots, peeled

1 cucumber

1 beet, greens removed

2 cups purified water

1. Place watercress, carrots, cucumber, beet, and 1 cup of water in a blender and blend until thoroughly combined.

2. Add remaining 1 cup of water while blending, as needed, until desired texture is achieved.

PER 1 CUP SERVING: Calories: 40 | Fat: 0g | Protein: 1g | Sodium: 55mg | Fiber: 2g | Carbohydrates: 9g

Taste the Rainbow for Optimal Health

It may be difficult to figure out which food group is best for your body and promoting its ideal functioning. The answer is . . . all of them! The easiest route to achieving optimum health is to taste the rainbow: Eat a variety of different foods with vibrant colors. By consuming a variety of fruits and vegetables with color, you can ensure your body is receiving abundant vitamins and nutrients. With variety comes the added benefit of never becoming tired of the same old fruit or veggie.

Apple Broccoli Detox Blend

Packed with fiber, vitamins, minerals, and phytochemicals that will clear out your digestive system, optimize brain functioning and mental clarity, and revitalize your body's many systems of operation, this recipe is a must have for detox!

INGREDIENTS | YIELDS 3–4 CUPS

1 cup romaine lettuce

2 apples, peeled and cored

1 cup broccoli

1 orange, peeled

⅛ cup parsley

2 cups purified water

1. Place romaine, apples, broccoli, orange, parsley, and 1 cup of water in a blender and blend until thoroughly combined.

2. Add remaining 1 cup of water while blending, as needed, until desired texture is achieved.

PER 1 CUP SERVING: Calories: 71 | Fat: 0g | Protein: 1g | Sodium: 12mg | Fiber: 3g | Carbohydrates: 18g

A Glad Gallbladder

A cleansed gallbladder is one free of toxins and waste and able to function properly and at an optimal level. Responsible for removing toxins and waste from the body along with the liver, the gallbladder is an important part of the body's makeup.

INGREDIENTS | YIELDS 3–4 CUPS

1 cup spinach

1 cup asparagus spears

½ lemon, peeled

1 tomato

1–2 cloves garlic, depending upon size

2 cups purified water

1. Place spinach, asparagus, lemon, tomato, garlic, and 1 cup water in a blender and blend until thoroughly combined.

2. Add remaining 1 cup of water while blending, as needed, until desired texture is achieved.

PER 1 CUP SERVING: Calories: 17 | Fat: 0g | Protein: 1g | Sodium: 11mg | Fiber: 1g | Carbohydrates: 4g

Why Does Gallbladder Health Matter?

Bile acids made in the liver and used by the small intestine for breaking down foods in digestion are stored in the gallbladder. If the gallbladder isn't functioning properly, digestion can be a difficult and painful process. By promoting a healthy gallbladder, you're ensuring the digestive process moves as smoothly and regularly as possible.

Cleanse Your Body with Sweet Citrus

Vitamin C does more than prevent illness, it also promotes great health!
This delicious combination of citrus fruits, watercress, and ginger make for a tasty way
to detoxify your body and promote health in one tasty treat!

INGREDIENTS | YIELDS 4–6 CUPS

1 cup watercress

2 cups pineapple, peeled and cored

1 orange, peeled

2 apples, peeled and cored

½" ginger, peeled

2 cups purified water

1. Place watercress, pineapple, orange, apples, ginger, and 1 cup of water in a blender and blend until thoroughly combined.

2. Add remaining 1 cup of water while blending, as needed, until desired texture is achieved.

PER 1 CUP SERVING: Calories: 99 | Fat: 0g | Protein: 1g | Sodium: 7mg | Fiber: 3g | Carbohydrates: 26g

Liven Up the Liver

The liver is a powerful organ responsible for removing unhealthy toxins from the body. Beet greens, beets, and apples are known to optimize liver functioning, and the addition of the banana's smooth texture makes this a healthy, tasty, liver-purifying blend.

INGREDIENTS | YIELDS 3–4 CUPS

1 cup beet greens

1 beet

3 apples, peeled and cored

1 banana, peeled

2 cups purified water

1. Place beet greens, beet, apples, banana, and 1 cup of water in a blender and blend until thoroughly combined.

2. Add remaining 1 cup of water while blending, as needed, until desired texture is achieved.

PER 1 CUP SERVING: Calories: 86 | Fat: 0g | Protein: 1g | Sodium: 24mg | Fiber: 3g | Carbohydrates: 23g

The Deep Colors of Detox

The vibrant colors of the kale, carrot, tomato, celery, and cucumber combine with potent garlic to develop an intensely flavored savory smoothie that provides a variety of vitamins and minerals and satisfies multiple vegetable servings in just one drink.

INGREDIENTS | YIELDS 3–4 CUPS

2 kale leaves

1 cucumber, peeled

2 celery stalks

1 carrot, peeled

1 tomato

1 garlic clove

2 cups purified water

1. Place kale, cucumber, celery, carrot, tomato, garlic, and 1 cup of water in a blender and blend until thoroughly combined.

2. Add remaining 1 cup of water while blending, as needed, until desired texture is achieved.

PER 1 CUP SERVING: Calories: 31 | Fat: 0g | Protein: 1g | Sodium: 39mg | Fiber: 2g | Carbohydrates: 6g

A Fruity Flush

*Ah, the refreshing flavors of fruits with the added benefits of a cleansed body—
not much can beat that! This is an easy and delicious way to satisfy cravings and fruit
and vegetable servings in the same smoothie.*

INGREDIENTS | YIELDS 3–4 CUPS

1 cup watercress

1 cucumber, peeled

½ cantaloupe, rind and seeds removed

1 pear, cored

1 banana, peeled

2 cups purified water

1. Place watercress, cucumber, cantaloupe, pear, banana, and 1 cup of water in a blender and blend until thoroughly combined.

2. Add remaining 1 cup of water while blending, as needed, until desired texture is achieved.

PER 1 CUP SERVING: Calories: 82 | Fat: 0g | Protein: 2g | Sodium: 19mg | Fiber: 3g | Carbohydrates: 21g

Refreshing Reprieve

*Refreshing flavors can keep a detoxifying diet on track. Calming cravings for sweets
or salty foods can keep your focus on your health rather than the unhealthy alternatives.*

INGREDIENTS | YIELDS 3–4 CUPS

1 cup romaine lettuce

1 apple, peeled and cored

1 cucumber, peeled

1 celery stalk

1 carrot, peeled

1 garlic clove

2 cups purified water

1. Place romaine, apple, cucumber, celery, carrot, garlic, and 1 cup water in a blender and blend until thoroughly combined.

2. Add remaining 1 cup of water while blending, as needed, until desired texture is achieved.

PER 1 CUP SERVING: Calories: 35 | Fat: 0g | Protein: 1g | Sodium: 15mg | Fiber: 2g | Carbohydrates: 8g

CHAPTER 9

Smoothies for Health and Disease Prevention

Pomegranate Preventer

Packed with vitamins and minerals that promote health and fight illness, blending these delicious fruits and vegetables is a tasty way to maintain great health.

INGREDIENTS | YIELDS 3–4 CUPS

1 cup iceberg lettuce

2 cups pomegranate pips

1 orange, peeled

1 banana, peeled

1 cup purified water

1. Place iceberg, pomegranate, orange, banana, and ½ cup water in a blender and blend until thoroughly combined.

2. Add remaining ½ cup water as needed while blending until desired consistency is achieved.

PER 1 CUP SERVING: Calories: 123 | Fat: 1g | Protein: 2g | Sodium: 6mg | Fiber: 6g | Carbohydrates: 29g

Cantaloupe for Cancer Prevention

The vibrant color of cantaloupe is from the abundant levels of beta-carotene, known for providing health benefits. Not only a sweet treat, this smoothie provides a wide variety of vitamins and minerals that work hard in preventing illness and disease.

INGREDIENTS | YIELDS 3–4 CUPS

1 cup watercress

½ cantaloupe, rind and seeds removed

1 apple, peeled and cored

1 banana, peeled

¼" ginger, peeled

1 cup purified water

1. Place watercress, cantaloupe, apple, banana, ginger, and ½ cup water in a blender and blend until thoroughly combined.

2. Add remaining ½ cup water as needed while blending until desired consistency is achieved.

PER 1 CUP SERVING: Calories: 70 | Fat: 0g | Protein: 1g | Sodium: 16mg | Fiber: 2g | Carbohydrates: 18g

Beta-Carotene's Fight Against Cancer

Among the many benefits beta-carotene offers, one of the major responsibilities of this strong antioxidant is to combat free radicals from the environment, certain foods, and unhealthy lifestyles. Free radicals can cause abnormal growth in cells, which can lead to dangerous illnesses like cancer. Studies have shown that diets rich in carotenes promote proper cell growth, thereby reducing the chances of cancers and disease.

Breathe Easy with Blackberries

Delicious blackberries are made even more tasty with the addition of lemon and ginger in this recipe. This smoothie packs a healthy dose of much-needed vitamins and minerals, and is rich and satisfying with the addition of protein-packed yogurt.

INGREDIENTS | YIELDS 3–4 CUPS

1 cup watercress

2 pints blackberries

1 banana, peeled

½ lemon, peeled

½" ginger, peeled

1 cup Greek-style yogurt

1. Place watercress, blackberries, banana, lemon, ginger, and ½ cup of yogurt in a blender and blend until thoroughly combined.

2. Add remaining ½ cup yogurt as needed while blending until desired consistency is achieved.

PER 1 CUP SERVING: Calories: 125 | Fat: 1g | Protein: 8g | Sodium: 29mg | Fiber: 9g | Carbohydrates: 25g

Blackberries Promote Respiratory Relief

Rich blackberries are not just a tasty treat, they are also packed with a variety of vitamins and minerals that can aid in overall health. Specifically, the magnesium content in blackberries is what makes it a crusader in promoting respiratory ease. Best known for its ability to relax the muscles and thin mucus most commonly associated with breathing difficulties, blackberries are an important addition to those in need of breathing assistance.

A Sweet Step to Great Health

Vitamins K and C, beta-carotenes, potassium, folate, and protein are rich in this delicious smoothie.
A one-stop shop for many of your fruit and vegetable servings,
this delicious recipe satisfies your sweet tooth and dietary needs.

INGREDIENTS | YIELDS 3–4 CUPS

1 cup romaine lettuce

1 cup pineapple, peeled and cored

1 pint strawberries

1 banana, peeled

1 cup Greek-style yogurt

1. Place romaine, pineapple, strawberries, banana, and ½ cup yogurt in a blender and blend until thoroughly combined.

2. Add remaining ½ cup yogurt as needed while blending until desired consistency is achieved.

PER 1 CUP SERVING: Calories: 108 | Fat: 0g | Protein: 7g | Sodium: 26mg | Fiber: 3g | Carbohydrates: 21g

Berries and Bananas for Bone Health

The crisp taste of iceberg lettuce is beautifully balanced with the addition of citrus, blackberries, bananas, and yogurt for a flavor combination that will make you enjoy eating better for your health.

INGREDIENTS | YIELDS 3–4 CUPS

1 cup iceberg lettuce

1 pint blackberries

1 cup pineapple, peeled and cored

2 bananas, peeled

1 cup Greek-style yogurt

Magnesium for Bone Health

The magnesium in blackberries can do amazing things for respiratory relief, but can also help create stronger bones. Playing an important role in the absorption of calcium, a diet rich in this powerful mineral ensures strong bones. Diets deficient in magnesium have also shown to prevent the body's proper use of estrogen, which can spell disaster for many of the body's cancer-fighting abilities.

1. Place iceberg, blackberries, pineapple, bananas, and ½ cup yogurt in a blender and blend until thoroughly combined.

2. Add remaining ½ cup yogurt as needed while blending until desired consistency is achieved.

PER 1 CUP SERVING: Calories: 137 | Fat: 1g | Protein: 8g | Sodium: 27mg | Fiber: 6g | Carbohydrates: 29g

A Grape Way to Bone Health

The sweetness of this smoothie just can't be beat! This recipe provides abundant vitamins and minerals with the added benefit of an amazingly refreshing taste.

INGREDIENTS | YIELDS 3–4 CUPS

1 cup watercress

2 cups red grapes

2 pears, cored

1 banana, peeled

1 cup purified water

Grapes' Anthocyanins and Proanthocyanins

You may never have heard of these two amazing compounds, but they are extremely important in promoting strong bones and optimizing bone health. Anthocyanins and proanthocyanins are compounds found in cells, and their duty is to ensure the bone structure is stabilized and to promote the collagen-building process that is absolutely imperative for strong bones. The two main foods packed with these strong compounds are deep-red and purple grapes and blueberries.

1. Place watercress, grapes, pears, banana, and ½ cup of water in a blender and blend until thoroughly combined.

2. Add remaining ½ cup of water as needed while blending until desired consistency is achieved.

PER 1 CUP SERVING: Calories: 131 | Fat: 0g | Protein: 1g | Sodium: 7mg | Fiber: 4g | Carbohydrates: 34g

Vitamin C Cancer Prevention

This vitamin C–packed recipe is a delicious blend of grapefruit, pineapple, and orange, intensified by the addition of ginger and vitamin K- and iron-rich spinach.

INGREDIENTS | YIELDS 3–4 CUPS

1 cup spinach

1 grapefruit, peeled

1 cup pineapple, peeled and cored

1 orange, peeled

½" ginger, peeled

1 cup purified water

1. Place spinach, grapefruit, pineapple, orange, ginger, and ½ cup water in a blender and blend until thoroughly combined.

2. Add remaining ½ cup water as needed while blending until desired consistency is achieved.

PER 1 CUP SERVING: Calories: 62 | Fat: 0g | Protein: 1g | Sodium: 8mg | Fiber: 2g | Carbohydrates: 16g

The Amazing Power of C

Not only is this strong vitamin the most well known for illness prevention, it works absolute wonders in many areas of promoting optimal health. In addition to being a strong supporter of bone health by improving the collagen-building process, building and retaining quality muscle, and improving the efficiency of blood vessels, it actually aids in the body's absorption of iron. Common mineral deficiencies can be reversed by including an abundance of vitamin C with your daily intake of iron-rich foods.

A Cool Blend for Diabetes

Maintaining a diet that optimizes sugar levels to ensure diabetic health is easy with this delicious blend. The combination of ingredients makes a refreshing treat that will keep you going when you need a boost.

INGREDIENTS | YIELDS 3–4 CUPS

1 cup watercress

1 celery stalk

1 cucumber, peeled

2 pears, cored

2 tablespoons mint

1 cup Greek-style yogurt

1. Place watercress, celery, cucumber, pears, mint, and ½ cup yogurt in a blender and blend until thoroughly combined.

2. Add remaining ½ cup yogurt as needed while blending until desired consistency is achieved.

PER 1 CUP SERVING: Calories: 94 | Fat: 0g | Protein: 7g | Sodium: 38mg | Fiber: 4g | Carbohydrates: 18g

Cherry Vanilla Respiratory Relief

Move over ice cream! This delicious smoothie will have you wondering, "Where are the greens?" Although the overpowering flavors of cherry and vanilla take center stage, the vitamin and mineral content of all of the ingredients (including the spinach) will do your body a world of good.

INGREDIENTS | YIELDS 3–4 CUPS

1 cup spinach
2 cups cherries, pitted
1 apple, peeled and cored
Pulp of 1 vanilla bean
½" ginger, peeled
2 cups purified water

1. Place spinach, cherries, apple, vanilla, ginger, and 1 cup water in a blender and blend until thoroughly combined.

2. Add remaining 1 cup of water as needed while blending until desired consistency is achieved.

PER 1 CUP SERVING: Calories: 73 | Fat: 0g | Protein: 1g | Sodium: 9mg | Fiber: 2g | Carbohydrates: 18g

The Breathing Benefit of Cherries

The abundant phytochemical content in cherries is what lends a hand in breathing. Phytochemicals make an impact on inflammation everywhere in the body. Commonly suggested for patients suffering from inflammation of joints, cherries can also assist in reducing the inflammation of airways and respiratory-related muscles. By including these powerful antioxidant- and vitamin-rich berries in your diet, you'll fight off illnesses that make breathing difficult and promote a more efficient respiratory process.

The Sweet Sensation of Health

If your diet and lifestyle leave you feeling in need of refreshment and vitality, this smoothie is for you. Hydrating melon and citrus combine with rich greens to provide a revitalizing lift.

INGREDIENTS | YIELDS 3–4 CUPS

1 cup watercress

2 cups watermelon

1 cup pineapple, peeled and cored

1 cup kefir

The Body's Need for Water

Cravings, fatigue, lack of focus, and derailed bodily functions can all result from not getting adequate water. The minimum recommended water intake is eight 8-ounce glasses of water daily, but those who exercise require even more. In addition to the water added while blending, the fruits and vegetable in this smoothie deliver one tasty way to increase your hydration.

1. Place watercress, watermelon, pineapple, and ¾ cup kefir in a blender and blend until thoroughly combined.

2. Add remaining ¼ cup kefir as needed while blending until desired consistency is achieved.

PER 1 CUP SERVING: Calories: 83 | Fat: 2g | Protein: 3g | Sodium: 36mg | Fiber: 1g | Carbohydrates: 14g

Apple Celery for Hydration

The fruits and greens in this smoothie provide natural sugars and carbohydrates, and celery regulates water levels.

INGREDIENTS | YIELDS 3–4 CUPS

1 cup romaine lettuce

3 Granny Smith apples, peeled and cored

2 celery stalks

¼" ginger, peeled

2 cups purified water

1. Place romaine, apples, celery, ginger, and 1 cup of water in a blender and blend until thoroughly combined.

2. Add remaining 1 cup of water as needed while blending until desired consistency is achieved.

PER 1 CUP SERVING: Calories: 64 | Fat: 0g | Protein: 1g | Sodium: 19mg | Fiber: 2g | Carbohydrates: 17g

"Pea" Is for Prevention

Sweetening this smoothie with sweet green peas makes a delightful treat. This tasty blend of watercress, cucumbers, and peas delivers a refreshing and filling snack with amazing health benefits from all of the rich ingredients.

INGREDIENTS | YIELDS 3–4 CUPS

1 cup watercress

2 cucumbers, peeled

1 cup petite sweet green peas

2 cups purified water

1. Place watercress, cucumbers, peas, and 1 cup of water in a blender and blend until thoroughly combined.

2. Add remaining 1 cup of water as needed while blending until desired consistency is achieved.

PER 1 CUP SERVING: Calories: 39 | Fat: 0g | Protein: 3g | Sodium: 44mg | Fiber: 2g | Carbohydrates: 7g

The Power of a Pea

Adding just 1 cup of this sweet veggie to your daily diet will provide over 50 percent of your daily recommended intake of vitamin K, along with vitamins B and C, manganese, folate, fiber, and protein. This results in stronger bones; heightened disease prevention; efficient metabolism of carbohydrates, fats, and proteins; improved cardiac health; and more energy.

Gear Up with Garlic

This savory smoothie makes a delicious meal replacement for an invigorating breakfast, satisfying lunch, or delightful dinner. The strong flavors of spinach and garlic combine with the cucumber, tomato, and celery for a taste sensation to savor.

INGREDIENTS | YIELDS 3–4 CUPS

1 cup spinach

1 cucumber, peeled

1 celery stalk

1 tomato

2–3 garlic cloves, depending upon size

2 cups purified water

1. Place spinach, cucumber, celery, tomato, garlic, and 1 cup water in a blender and blend until thoroughly combined.

2. Add remaining 1 cup of water as needed while blending until desired consistency is achieved.

PER 1 CUP SERVING: Calories: 17 | Fat: 0g | Protein: 1g | Sodium: 19mg | Fiber: 1g | Carbohydrates: 3g

Garlic Prep for Optimal Benefits

Cooking garlic for as little as 60 seconds has shown to cause it to lose some of its anticancer properties. Packed with an abundance of vitamins, minerals, and nutrients that work hard to fight cancer and heart disease, prevent bacterial and viral infections, improve iron metabolism, control blood pressure, and act as an anti-inflammatory, garlic's abilities can be optimized by crushing or chopping it and preparing it without heat.

Romaine to the Rescue!

*Crisp romaine, broccoli, carrots, garlic, and ginger combine in this recipe
to make for one satisfying, savory smoothie that will promote health for your eyes,
digestion, muscle repair, and mental clarity.*

INGREDIENTS | YIELDS 3–4 CUPS

2 cups romaine lettuce

½ cup broccoli

2 carrots

1 garlic clove

½" ginger, peeled

2 cups purified water

1. Place romaine, broccoli, carrots, garlic, ginger, and 1 cup of water in a blender and blend until thoroughly combined.

2. Add remaining 1 cup of water as needed while blending until desired consistency is achieved.

PER 1 CUP SERVING: Calories: 22 | Fat: 0g | Protein: 1g | Sodium: 29mg | Fiber: 2g | Carbohydrates: 5g

A Peppery Way to Promote Health

*Arugula and red pepper join forces with crisp celery and garlic
for a spicy treat with a bite in this smoothie.*

INGREDIENTS | YIELDS 3–4 CUPS

1 cup arugula

2 celery stalks

½ red bell pepper, cored with ribs intact

1 garlic clove

1½ cups water

1. Place arugula, celery, red pepper, garlic, and ¾ cup of the water in a blender and blend until thoroughly combined.

2. Add remaining ¾ cup of the water as needed while blending until desired consistency is achieved.

PER 1 CUP SERVING: Calories: 14 | Fat: 0g | Protein: 1g |
Sodium: 26mg | Fiber: 1g | Carbohydrates: 3g

Garlic and Onions Keep the Doctor Away

Although it will probably keep more people away than just the doctor, garlic and onions make for an amazing taste combination that will surprise any green-smoothie skeptic. The watercress, celery, and zucchini downplay the intense flavors of the garlic and onions.

INGREDIENTS | YIELDS 3–4 CUPS

1 cup watercress

1 celery stalk

1 green onion

1 zucchini

1 clove garlic

2 cups purified water

1. Place watercress, celery, onion, zucchini, garlic, and 1 cup of water in a blender and blend until thoroughly combined.

2. Add remaining 1 cup of water as needed while blending until desired consistency is achieved.

PER 1 CUP SERVING: Calories: 13 | Fat: 0g | Protein: 1g | Sodium: 19mg | Fiber: 1g | Carbohydrates: 3g

Celery for Diabetic Health

To waken your senses in the early morning or even in the mid-afternoon, these powerful antioxidant-rich ingredients work together to provide energy, renewed vitality, and overall health.

INGREDIENTS | YIELDS 5–6 CUPS

1 cup arugula

1 celery stalk

1 tomato

½ red bell pepper, cored with ribs intact

1 green onion

1 garlic clove

⅛ cup parsley

2 cups purified water

1. Place arugula, celery, tomato, red pepper, onion, garlic, parsley, and 1 cup of water in a blender and blend until thoroughly combined.

2. Add remaining 1 cup of water as needed while blending until desired consistency is achieved.

PER 1 CUP SERVING: Calories: 13 | Fat: 0g | Protein: 1g | Sodium: 13mg | Fiber: 1g | Carbohydrates: 3g

The Importance of Celery for Diabetics

The sodium content in this crisp veggie plays an important role in a diabetic's diet. By consuming this delicious vegetable, the body is more efficient in regulating and maintaining water balance. Celery is rich in vitamins A, C, K, B6, and B1 as well as calcium, potassium, fiber, and folate, and is also a natural diuretic.

Spice It Up!

The arugula, onion, and pepper combine in this recipe for a powerfully delicious treat. Mushrooms are a woody ingredient that tones down the peppery flavor of arugula.

INGREDIENTS | YIELDS 3–4 CUPS

1 cup arugula

1 green onion

½ red bell pepper, cored

½ cup mushrooms, stems intact

2 cups purified water

1. Place arugula, onion, red pepper, mushrooms, and 1 cup of water in a blender and blend until thoroughly combined.

2. Add remaining 1 cup of water as needed while blending until desired consistency is achieved.

PER 1 CUP SERVING: Calories: 14 | Fat: 0g | Protein: 1g | Sodium: 8mg | Fiber: 1g | Carbohydrates: 3g

Red Bell Peppers and Vitamins C and A

This beautiful vegetable not only provides a tasty crunch to salads and entrées, it also provides a whopping dose of both vitamins A and C. Providing almost 300 percent of your recommended daily amount of vitamin C and just over 100 percent of your recommended daily amount of vitamin A, it prevents illnesses like cancer, heart disease, and influenza and protects against free radicals that can cause aged-looking skin, increased fatigue, and zapped energy and mental focus.

Pear Prevention

This refreshing smoothie makes a great snack when your body and mind need a lift. The sweet pears, spicy ginger, and rich cabbage and celery combine with the cooling cucumber for an overall refreshing blend.

INGREDIENTS | YIELDS 3–4 CUPS

1 cup green cabbage

3 pears, cored

1 cucumber, peeled

1 celery stalk

½" ginger, peeled

1 cup kefir

1. Place cabbage, pears, cucumber, celery, ginger, and ½ cup kefir in a blender and blend until thoroughly combined.

2. Add remaining ½ cup kefir as needed while blending until desired consistency is achieved.

PER 1 CUP SERVING: Calories: 132 | Fat: 2g | Protein: 3g | Sodium: 46mg | Fiber: 6g | Carbohydrates: 27g

Health's No Joke with Artichokes

Although artichokes are most commonly used in dips, salads, and entrées, raw artichokes make for a tasty addition to green-smoothie recipes such as this one. Artichokes pack a protective punch against disease, inflammation, and bone loss.

INGREDIENTS | YIELDS 3–4 CUPS

1 cup spinach
4 artichoke hearts
1 green onion
2 celery stalks
2 cups purified water

1. Place spinach, artichokes, onion, celery, and 1 cup of water in a blender and blend until thoroughly combined.

2. Add remaining 1 cup of water as needed while blending until desired consistency is achieved.

PER 1 CUP SERVING: Calories: 59 | Fat: 0g | Protein: 4g | Sodium: 130mg | Fiber: 7g | Carbohydrates: 13g

Turnip Turnaround

*Turnips are most often seen roasted with other root vegetables around the holidays,
but most would never think to include them in a green smoothie.
The turnip and carrots make for a delicious taste combination.*

INGREDIENTS | YIELDS 3–4 CUPS

1 cup watercress

2 turnips, peeled and cut to fit blender

3 carrots, peeled

2 celery stalks

2 cups purified water

1. Place watercress, turnips, carrots, celery, and 1 cup of water in a blender and blend until thoroughly combined.

2. Add remaining 1 cup of water as needed while blending until desired consistency is achieved.

PER 1 CUP SERVING: Calories: 40 | Fat: 0g | Protein: 1g | Sodium: 94mg | Fiber: 3g | Carbohydrates: 9g

CHAPTER 10

Smoothies for Weight Loss

Luscious Lemon

Lemon is a refreshing ingredient and is packed with vitamin C. Not only does this vitamin aid in building immunity, it plays an important role in the metabolism of fat!

INGREDIENTS | YIELDS 3–4 CUPS

1 cup watercress

2 lemons, peeled

2 celery stalks

2 cucumbers, peeled

½" ginger, peeled

2 cups purified water

1. Place watercress, lemons, celery, cucumbers, ginger, and 1 cup of water in a blender and blend until thoroughly combined.

2. Add remaining 1 cup of water as needed while blending until desired consistency is achieved.

PER 1 CUP SERVING: Calories: 25 | Fat: 0g | Protein: 1g | Sodium: 25mg | Fiber: 2g | Carbohydrates: 6g

Green Tea Metabolism Booster

Green tea is packed with fat-burning catechin antioxidants that aid in weight loss. Using green tea instead of water in this smoothie amplifies the fat-burning properties of the vitamin- and mineral-rich greens and fruits.

INGREDIENTS | YIELDS 3–4 CUPS

1 cup watercress

1 lemon, peeled

2 cups cantaloupe, rind and seeds removed

1 cup raspberries

2 cups green tea

Making Quick Green Tea

Most people who are on the go prefer to make their green tea with the conveniently prepackaged tea bags. By purchasing quality green tea bags and using quality purified and filtered water, you can make your own fat-burning green tea on the go, at the office, or even in the car. Boil the water and pour it into a safe (preferably glass) container, steep the tea bag for the suggested amount of time to maximize antioxidant release and taste, and enjoy!

1. Place watercress, lemon, cantaloupe, raspberries, and 1 cup of tea in a blender and blend until thoroughly combined.

2. Add remaining 1 cup of tea as needed while blending until desired consistency is achieved.

PER 1 CUP SERVING: Calories: 49 | Fat: 0g | Protein: 1g | Sodium: 17mg | Fiber: 3g | Carbohydrates: 12g

Cantaloupe Creation

Cantaloupe is rich in vitamins and minerals important for weight loss and maximizing metabolic rates. A tasty treat for breakfast, lunch, or dinner, this satisfying combination of delightful flavors makes for a great fat-burning meal replacement.

INGREDIENTS | YIELDS 3–4 CUPS

1 cup watercress

½ cantaloupe, rind and seeds removed

1 cup pineapple, peeled and cored

1 orange, peeled

½" ginger, peeled

2 cups green tea

1. Place watercress, cantaloupe, pineapple, orange, ginger, and 1 cup of tea in a blender and blend until thoroughly combined.

2. Add remaining 1 cup of tea as needed while blending until desired consistency is achieved.

PER 1 CUP SERVING: Calories: 67 | Fat: 0g | Protein: 1g | Sodium: 15mg | Fiber: 2g | Carbohydrates: 17g

Cantaloupe for Regulating Metabolism

Anyone who struggles with weight loss and management knows the downfalls of a slow metabolism. Affected by sleep, stress, diet, and activity levels, metabolism can be increased not only through lifestyle but also the foods we choose. Cantaloupe and other fruits and veggies high in vitamin C play an important role in regulating and optimizing metabolism, making weight loss and management more successful.

Beet the Bloat

Beets are high in vitamins, minerals, and antioxidants that promote your body's ability to function optimally. By combining beets with apples, lemon, ginger, and green tea, you can fuel your body with the nutrients it needs while optimizing its fat-burning potential.

INGREDIENTS | YIELDS 3–4 CUPS

1 cup beet greens

1 beet

3 apples, peeled and cored

½ lemon, peeled

¼" ginger, peeled

2 cups green tea

1. Place beet greens, beet, apples, lemon, and ginger with 1 cup tea in a blender and blend until thoroughly combined.

2. Add remaining 1 cup of tea as needed while blending until desired consistency is achieved.

PER 1 CUP SERVING: Calories: 73 | Fat: 0g | Protein: 1g | Sodium: 38mg | Fiber: 3g | Carbohydrates: 19g

Slim Down with This Sweet Treat

This smoothie will satisfy any craving while delivering loads of vitamins and nutrients for optimizing your energy and stamina. It makes an amazing meal or snack that will energize your body and mind while keeping your diet on track.

INGREDIENTS | YIELDS 3–4 CUPS

1 cup spinach

2 red apples, peeled and cored

2 pears, cored

½ lemon, peeled

¼" ginger, peeled

2 cups green tea

1. Place spinach, apples, pears, lemon, ginger, and 1 cup of tea in a blender and blend until thoroughly combined.

2. Add remaining 1 cup of tea as needed while blending until desired consistency is achieved.

PER 1 CUP SERVING: Calories: 96 | Fat: 0g | Protein: 1g | Sodium: 7mg | Fiber: 4g | Carbohydrates: 25g

Benefits of Natural Carbs

The calories in fruits and vegetables are used in digestion and by body processes that function to perform normal activity, so there is virtually no waste of calories and none to be stored as fat. In addition, the carbohydrates of fruits and vegetables turn to sugars more slowly than refined carbohydrates, allowing them to burn fat without fluctuating blood sugar levels.

Colors of Success

By combining a variety of vibrant colors in your diet, you can ensure you're providing a variety of vitamins and minerals your body requires to run at its optimal level. The ingredients of this smoothie make a tasty treat for your eyes and your body.

INGREDIENTS | YIELDS 4–6 CUPS

1 cup beet greens

1 beet

3 carrots, peeled

2 apples, cored

1 banana, peeled

3 cups green tea

1. Place beet greens, beet, carrots, apples, banana, and 1½ cups of tea in a blender and blend until thoroughly combined.

2. Add remaining 1½ cups tea as needed while blending until desired consistency is achieved.

PER 1 CUP SERVING: Calories: 70 | Fat: 0g | Protein: 1g | Sodium: 47mg | Fiber: 3g | Carbohydrates: 18g

Cinch Pounds with Citrus

This sweet combination of greens and citrus makes for a refreshing snack for your body and mind. This smoothie stimulates your brain for improved mental clarity and focus, your body for more efficient metabolism, and your overall health with the abundance of vitamins and minerals.

INGREDIENTS | YIELDS 3–4 CUPS

1 cup watercress

1 grapefruit, peeled

½ pineapple, peeled and cored

1 orange, peeled

½ lemon, peeled

½ lime, peeled

2 cups green tea

1. Place watercress, grapefruit, pineapple, orange, lemon, lime, and 1 cup of tea in a blender and blend until thoroughly combined.

2. Add remaining 1 cup of tea as needed while blending until desired consistency is achieved.

PER 1 CUP SERVING: Calories: 104 | Fat: 0g | Protein: 2g | Sodium: 5mg | Fiber: 2g | Carbohydrates: 27g

Vitamin C

Some restrictive diets can leave your body feeling fatigued and your mind fuzzy. With those side effects, it's no wonder so many people abandon their diet plans! With an increase in vitamin C in your daily diet, your body's metabolism of proteins, fats, and carbohydrates improves, making for wonderful effects in mental clarity, improved energy and stamina, and a better feeling of fullness from your foods. It also improves the body's ability to remove toxins and waste.

Apple Pie for Weight Loss

Even the most avid dieter who sticks to every aspect of her diet gets hit with cravings now and again. This smoothie will satisfy your taste buds' desire for delicious apple pie without the unhealthy sugars, carbs, and lack of nutrition of the traditional treat.

INGREDIENTS | YIELDS 3–4 CUPS

1 cup watercress

3 Granny Smith apples, peeled and cored

½ lemon, peeled

1 teaspoon cloves

½" ginger, peeled

2 cups green tea

1. Place watercress, apples, lemon, cloves, ginger, and 1 cup of tea in a blender and blend until thoroughly combined.

2. Add remaining 1 cup of tea as needed while blending until desired consistency is achieved.

PER 1 CUP SERVING: Calories: 65 | Fat: 0g | Protein: 1g | Sodium: 5mg | Fiber: 2g | Carbohydrates: 17g

A Smart Way to Satisfy Cravings

A smart suggestion for diet success is to consume water or healthy fruits and vegetables when cravings strike. Green smoothies are an excellent option because they provide a large dose of greens, fruits, and vegetables tailored to fit your craving. Sweet smoothies can provide the sugar you're craving, and the savory options work wonders in calming your want for salt.

Smooth Carrot Apple

The delightfully sweet combination of carrots and apples downplays the spinach. Intensifying the effects of weight loss, the lemon and green tea act to fuel your body's fat-burning furnace!

INGREDIENTS | YIELDS 3–4 CUPS

1 cup spinach

3 carrots

2 apples, peeled and cored

1 banana, peeled

½ lemon, peeled

2 cups green tea

1. Place spinach, carrots, apples, banana, lemon, and 1 cup of tea in a blender and blend until thoroughly combined.

2. Add remaining 1 cup of tea as needed while blending until desired consistency is achieved.

PER 1 CUP SERVING: Calories: 89 | Fat: 0g | Protein: 1g | Sodium: 38mg | Fiber: 3g | Carbohydrates: 23g

Sweet Ginger Melon

Cantaloupe and watermelon are a hydrating pair in this smoothie.
Refreshing your body while providing loads of vitamins and minerals,
these super fruits lend important water content, a must have for successful diets.

INGREDIENTS | YIELDS 3–4 CUPS

1 cup watercress

½ cantaloupe, rind and seeds removed

1 cup watermelon

½" ginger, peeled

1 cup green tea

1. Place watercress, cantaloupe, watermelon, ginger, and ½ cup tea in a blender and blend until thoroughly combined.

2. Add remaining ½ cup tea as needed while blending until desired consistency is achieved.

PER 1 CUP SERVING: Calories: 38 | Fat: 0g | Protein: 1g | Sodium: 15mg | Fiber: 1g | Carbohydrates: 9g

The Importance of Water in Dieting

Hunger, fatigue, and lack of focus can be terrible side effects of not providing your body with adequate water. Especially in restrictive diets that provide little water from foods, the importance of consuming adequate water is tenfold! If the blandness of water makes consuming the recommended amount unbearable, opt for green tea. If you prefer fruit juices, green smoothies with loads of fruits make a healthier option with far less sugar, preservatives, and additives.

Gorgeous Greens for a Gorgeous Body

*These gorgeous green fruits and veggies make a deliciously refreshing treat.
Not only is this a filling smoothie option, the ingredients offer balanced nutrition, vitamins,
minerals, and antioxidants that will keep you moving throughout your day.*

INGREDIENTS | YIELDS 3–4 CUPS

1 cup spinach

2 Granny Smith apples, peeled and cored

2 celery stalks

1 cucumber, peeled

½ lime, peeled

2 cups green tea

1. Place spinach, apples, celery, cucumber, lime, and 1 cup of tea in a blender and blend until thoroughly combined.

2. Add remaining 1 cup of tea as needed while blending until desired consistency is achieved.

PER 1 CUP SERVING: Calories: 53 | Fat: 0g | Protein: 1g | Sodium: 23mg | Fiber: 2g | Carbohydrates: 14g

Total Health Inside and Out

The natural nutrition found in greens and fruits can do wonders for your body on the inside and out! Consuming deep greens, vibrant fruits and veggies; hydrating with purified water; and daily exercising combine for health benefits you can see and feel.

Asparagus Carrot

Asparagus is a well-known diuretic that works wonders on those days when the scale says one thing and your jeans say another. A great light meal or satisfying snack, this smoothie will fill you up without weighing you down!

INGREDIENTS | YIELDS 3–4 CUPS

1 cup watercress
1 cup asparagus
3 carrots, peeled
1 celery stalk
1 garlic clove
2 cups purified water

1. Place watercress, asparagus, carrots, celery, garlic, and 1 cup water in a blender and blend until thoroughly combined.

2. Add remaining 1 cup of water as needed while blending until desired consistency is achieved.

PER 1 CUP SERVING: Calories: 29 | Fat: 0g | Protein: 1g | Sodium: 46mg | Fiber: 2g | Carbohydrates: 6g

A Spicy Blue Blast

Antioxidant-rich blueberries and fat-burning blackberries pair up with soothing ginger for a refreshingly light smoothie that will make any diet more enjoyable! These sweet ingredients can even be enjoyed as a midnight snack without the guilt of the alternatives.

INGREDIENTS | YIELDS 3–4 CUPS

1 cup watercress
2 cups blueberries
1 cup blackberries
½" ginger, peeled
2 cups green tea

1. Place watercress, berries, ginger, and 1 cup tea in a blender and blend until thoroughly combined.

2. Add remaining 1 cup of green tea as needed while blending until desired consistency is achieved.

PER 1 CUP SERVING: Calories: 60 | Fat: 0g | Protein: 1g | Sodium: 5mg | Fiber: 4g | Carbohydrates: 15g

Magic Berries

Blueberries, blackberries, strawberries, and raspberries are superfoods disguised as sweet treats. These fat-burning fruits are low in calories, packed with antioxidants that promote weight loss, and supply quick energy that also allows you to burn fat fast. They are also rich in magnesium, one of the most important minerals when dieting, key to promoting energy regulation.

Ginger Apple Berry

With the fiber of the greens and apples, the vitamin C and antioxidants of the berries, and the soothing effect of the ginger, this recipe makes for the perfect combination for optimizing digestion. Any stomach discomfort can be alleviated with this tasty combo!

INGREDIENTS | YIELDS 3–4 CUPS

1 cup watercress
1 cup strawberries
2 apples, cored
½" ginger, peeled
2 cups green tea

1. Place watercress, strawberries, apples, ginger, and 1 cup tea in a blender and blend until thoroughly combined.

2. Add remaining 1 cup of tea as needed while blending until desired consistency is achieved.

PER 1 CUP SERVING: Calories: 62 | Fat: 0g | Protein: 1g | Sodium: 5mg | Fiber: 3g | Carbohydrates: 16g

Savory Slim Down

With the savory smoothie options available, your desire for salty unhealthy alternatives can be satisfied healthfully. Enjoy this vitamin- and mineral-packed recipe for a savory and satisfying meal option that will deliver sound nutrition, great taste, and zero guilt.

INGREDIENTS | YIELDS 3–4 CUPS

1 cup spinach
1 cup asparagus
1 tomato
1 green onion
1 clove garlic
1½ cups purified water

1. Place spinach, asparagus, tomato, onion, garlic, and ¾ cup of the water in a blender and blend until thoroughly combined.

2. Add remaining ¾ cup of water as needed while blending until desired consistency is achieved.

PER 1 CUP SERVING: Calories: 22 | Fat: 0g | Protein: 2g | Sodium: 14mg | Fiber: 2g | Carbohydrates: 4g

Garlic Gets the Pounds Off

*In addition to delivering vitamins and minerals, antioxidants,
and an amazing amount of health benefits for your heart,
garlic provides an astounding amount of protection against illness.*

INGREDIENTS | YIELDS 3–4 CUPS

1 cup romaine lettuce

1 cup broccoli

1 celery stalk

1 tomato

1 green onion

2 cloves garlic

2 cups purified water

1. Place romaine, broccoli, celery, tomato, onion, and garlic with 1 cup of water in a blender and blend until thoroughly combined.

2. Add remaining 1 cup of water as needed while blending until desired consistency is achieved.

PER 1 CUP SERVING: Calories: 20 | Fat: 0g | Protein: 1g | Sodium: 21mg | Fiber: 1g | Carbohydrates: 4g

Minty Mango Metabolism Maximizer

The delightful flavors of watercress, mango, oranges, and green tea are intensified by the addition of mint in this recipe. This refreshing smoothie is sweet—but not too sweet.

INGREDIENTS | YIELDS 3–4 CUPS

1 cup watercress

1 cup mango, pitted

2 oranges, peeled

¼ cup mint leaves

1 cup green tea

1. Place watercress, mango, oranges, mint, and ½ cup of tea in a blender and blend until thoroughly combined.

2. Add remaining ½ cup of tea as needed while blending until desired consistency is achieved.

PER 1 CUP SERVING: Calories: 75 | Fat: 0g | Protein: 2g | Sodium: 7mg | Fiber: 4g | Carbohydrates: 19g

Zap Pounds with Zippy Zucchini

As a meal option, this smoothie combines intense flavors of filling ingredients that will provide sustainable energy and improved mental processes in a satisfying alternative to fattening, salt-laden savory entrées.

INGREDIENTS | YIELDS 3–4 CUPS

2 kale leaves

1 zucchini, peeled

1 cup asparagus

½ red bell pepper

1 green onion

2 garlic cloves

2 cups purified water

1. Place kale, zucchini, asparagus, red pepper, onion, garlic, and 1 cup water in a blender and blend until thoroughly combined.

2. Add remaining 1 cup of water as needed while blending until desired consistency is achieved.

PER 1 CUP SERVING: Calories: 31 | Fat: 0g | Protein: 2g | Sodium: 17mg | Fiber: 2g | Carbohydrates: 6g

Refresh That Body

When you're feeling dried out, tired, or just down, vitamin C–rich smoothies
like this one can give you automatic energy that will pick you up and keep you going.
Staying focused on your weight-loss goals is a lot easier when you feel refreshed.

INGREDIENTS | YIELDS 3–4 CUPS

1 cup watercress

½ cantaloupe, rind and seeds removed

1 cup strawberries

1 orange, peeled

½ lemon, peeled

1 cup green tea

1. Place watercress, cantaloupe, strawberries, orange, lemon, and ½ cup of tea in a blender and blend until thoroughly combined.

2. Add remaining green tea as needed while blending until desired consistency is achieved.

PER 1 CUP SERVING: Calories: 60 | Fat: 0g | Protein: 2g | Sodium: 15mg | Fiber: 3g | Carbohydrates: 15g

Vitamin C Deficiencies

Even though orange juice, fresh produce, and affordable fruits and vegetables packed with vitamin C are readily available and accessible to Americans, most don't get the recommended daily value of 60mg per day. Although multivitamins and vitamin C pill alternatives provide loads of vitamin C, the fresh sources of this important vitamin are a healthier, more refreshing option that can give you the added benefits of extra vitamins and minerals.

Flush Out Fat with Fiber

This fiber-rich recipe provides a tasty blend of fruits and veggies heightened with the addition of lemon and ginger. Important vitamins and nutrients are packed in the kale, apples, carrots, and lemon.

INGREDIENTS | YIELDS 3–4 CUPS

2 kale leaves

4 apples, peeled and cored

2 carrots, peeled

½ lemon, peeled

¼" ginger, peeled

3 cups green tea

1. Place kale, apples, carrots, lemon, ginger, and 1½ cups of the tea in a blender and blend until thoroughly combined.

2. Add remaining 1½ cups of tea as needed while blending until desired consistency is achieved.

PER 1 CUP SERVING: Calories: 102 | Fat: 0g | Protein: 1g | Sodium: 28mg | Fiber: 3g | Carbohydrates: 26g

Fiber for Fat Loss

Important additions to any weight-loss diet are fruits and vegetables packed with fiber. Not only does fiber help flush out toxins and waste products from the digestive system, it requires energy to digest. Calorie for calorie, fruits and veggies rich in fiber require more energy to digest than other foods lacking in this powerful nutrient. By consuming fiber-rich foods, you can provide your body with important vitamins and nutrients with calories that get used rather than stored.

Manage Your Weight with Mangoes

Delicious and nutritious, mangoes are a sweet fruit that provide loads of vitamin C and help optimize your fat-burning metabolism. This easy recipe combines only a few ingredients but delivers an amazing amount of nutrition for weight loss and total health.

INGREDIENTS | YIELDS 3–4 CUPS

1 cup watercress

2 cups mangoes, pitted and peeled

½ lemon, peeled

¼" ginger

1½ cups green tea

1. Place watercress, mangoes, lemon, ginger, and ¾ cup of the tea in a blender and blend until thoroughly combined.

2. Add remaining ¾ cup of tea as needed while blending until desired consistency is achieved.

PER 1 CUP SERVING: Calories: 72 | Fat: 0g | Protein: 1g | Sodium: 6mg | Fiber: 2g | Carbohydrates: 19g

Weight Loss Versus Total Health

Fad diets may help you lose those stubborn pounds fast, but can also make for an unhealthy body and mind when those lost pounds are regained following the return to "normal" foods. Eating a clean diet rich in vitamins and nutrients like those found in deep greens, fruits, veggies, and unprocessed foods can deliver healthy benefits for your body and mind now and years down the road! Improving all of your body's functions can make a huge difference in daily life and promote a longer, healthier, happier one!

CHAPTER 11

Smoothies for Athletes

Carrot Commando

Carrots, spinach, and apples combine for a delightfully sweet and filling smoothie.
They provide loads of important vitamins and minerals needed for optimal functioning
of all those body systems designed to make you move and help you move faster.

INGREDIENTS | YIELDS 3–4 CUPS

1 cup spinach

4 carrots, peeled

2 apples, peeled and cored

2 cups purified water

1. Place spinach, carrots, apples, and 1 cup of water in a blender and blend until thoroughly combined.

2. Add remaining 1 cup of water as needed while blending until desired consistency is achieved.

PER 1 CUP SERVING: Calories: 65 | Fat: 0g | Protein: 1g | Sodium: 50mg | Fiber: 3g | Carbohydrates: 16g

Carrots for Flushing an Athlete's Fat Stores

Among the many capabilities of carrots, one little-known responsibility is its assistance to the liver's cleansing power. Carrots aid the liver's cleansing process by keeping it squeaky clean and helping to more efficiently move excess bile and fat stores out of the body.

Rapid Recovery

Tasty and powerful, this recipe's ingredients provide powerful protein from intense vitamin- and mineral-rich veggies. The addition of the lemon and garlic benefit your body by promoting a healthy metabolic level for more efficient fat burning.

INGREDIENTS | YIELDS 3–4 CUPS

1 cup watercress

1 cup broccoli

1 celery stalk

½ lemon, peeled

1 garlic clove

2 cups Greek-style yogurt

1. Place watercress, broccoli, celery, lemon, garlic, and 1 cup of yogurt in a blender and blend until thoroughly combined.

2. Add remaining 1 cup of yogurt as needed while blending until desired consistency is achieved.

PER 1 CUP SERVING: Calories: 78 | Fat: 0g | Protein: 13g | Sodium: 67mg | Fiber: 1g | Carbohydrates: 7g

Yogurt for Rapid Recovery

You know protein delivers recovery aid to your muscles, but what is the best type to deliver maximum benefits and reap the most rewards? Chicken, beef, pork, and fish all come with saturated fats and aren't suitable for vegetarian athletes. If you're not interested in a protein shake of the powdered variety, turn to Greek-style yogurt! It has twice as much protein (20 grams), has lower carbs (9 grams or less), and half the sodium of regular yogurt.

Broccoli Blastoff

Broccoli and kale add a great dose of protein in this smoothie. If you're looking for even more protein, there is the delightful option of protein powders in a variety of flavors that would blend nicely with savory smoothies such as this.

INGREDIENTS | YIELDS 3–4 CUPS

2 kale leaves

1 cup broccoli

½ red bell pepper

2 celery stalks

1 green onion

1–2 garlic cloves, depending on size

2 cups purified water

1. Place kale, broccoli, pepper, celery, onion, garlic, and 1 cup of water in a blender and blend until thoroughly combined.

2. Add remaining 1 cup of water as needed while blending until desired consistency is achieved.

PER 1 CUP SERVING: Calories: 23 | Fat: 0g | Protein: 1g | Sodium: 18mg | Fiber: 1g | Carbohydrates: 1g

Zoom with Zucchini

The vibrant veggies and cayenne pepper in this recipe make a fat-burning, calorie-zapping smoothie that will fill you up and fire your engines!

INGREDIENTS | YIELDS 3–4 CUPS

1 cup spinach

1 zucchini

1 tomato

2 celery stalks

1 green onion

2 garlic cloves

⅛ teaspoon cayenne pepper

2 cups purified water

1. Place spinach, zucchini, tomato, celery, onion, garlic, cayenne, and 1 cup of water in a blender and blend until thoroughly combined.

2. Add remaining 1 cup of water as needed while blending until desired consistency is achieved.

PER 1 CUP SERVING: Calories: 22 | Fat: 0g | Protein: 1g | Sodium: 32mg | Fiber: 2g | Carbohydrates: 5g

Sweet Spinach Spinner

This sweet spin on vitamin-rich spinach makes a delightful treat you can enjoy before or after an exercise session. The low glycemic index of the ingredients makes a sustainable energy-powering blend of vitamins, minerals, and phytochemicals that will help you perform without the energy crash of caffeinated energy drinks.

INGREDIENTS | YIELDS 3–4 CUPS

1 cup spinach

4 apples, peeled and cored

¼" ginger, peeled

2 cups purified water

1. Place spinach, apples, ginger, and 1 cup of water in a blender and blend until thoroughly combined.

2. Add remaining 1 cup of water as needed while blending until desired consistency is achieved.

PER 1 CUP SERVING: Calories: 79 | Fat: 0g | Protein: 1g | Sodium: 8mg | Fiber: 2g | Carbohydrates: 21g

Powerful Parsnips

Packed with vitamin C, parsnips are a tasty ingredient in this surprisingly sweet smoothie. Packed with important minerals for energy and stamina, root veggies are a great way to maximize your smoothie's potency potential.

INGREDIENTS | YIELDS 3–4 CUPS

1 cup watercress

1 parsnip, peeled

3 carrots, peeled

2 cups purified water

1. Place watercress, parsnip, carrots, and 1 cup of water in a blender and blend until thoroughly combined.

2. Add remaining 1 cup of water as needed while blending until desired consistency is achieved.

PER 1 CUP SERVING: Calories: 31 | Fat: 0g | Protein: 1g | Sodium: 39mg | Fiber: 2g | Carbohydrates: 7g

Killer Kale Kickoff

Packed with an abundance of vitamin K, a fat-soluble compound,
kale is a healthy way to get your daily recommended amount of K in a one-stop shop.

INGREDIENTS | YIELDS 3–4 CUPS

2 kale leaves

4 carrots, peeled

1 cucumber, peeled

2 green onions

2 garlic cloves

2 cups purified water

1. Place kale, carrots, cucumber, onions, garlic, and 1 cup of water in a blender and blend until thoroughly combined.

2. Add remaining 1 cup of water as needed while blending until desired consistency is achieved.

PER 1 CUP SERVING: Calories: 43 | Fat: 0g | Protein: 2g | Sodium: 6mg | Fiber: 3g | Carbohydrates: 9g

Protein Packer

The creamy combination of sweet fruits and almonds blends beautifully with the crisp watercress for a protein-packed delight you're sure to enjoy after a strenuous workout.

INGREDIENTS | YIELDS 3–4 CUPS

¼ cup almonds

¾ cup purified water

1 cup watercress

1 apple, peeled and cored

1 banana, peeled

1 cup Greek-style yogurt

What Is Watercress?

This leafy green veggie is packed with vitamin C, calcium, and potassium, all important vitamins for maintaining a healthy immune system and providing structural support for the bones of an athlete. But that's not all! Its acid-forming minerals cleanse and normalize the intestines while the chlorophyll stimulates the metabolism and the circulatory system. Higher metabolism, better blood distribution, less illness and disease, and cleaner digestion are packed in a single serving of this amazing green leafy veggie!

1. Combine almonds and water in a blender and emulsify until no almond bits remain.

2. Add watercress, apple, banana, and ½ cup yogurt and blend until thoroughly combined with almond milk.

3. Add remaining ½ cup yogurt as needed while blending until desired consistency is achieved.

PER 1 CUP SERVING: Calories: 130 | Fat: 5g | Protein: 8g | Sodium: 29mg | Fiber: 2g | Carbohydrates: 16g

Collide with Collards

Refreshing and nutritious, this blend delivers powerful vitamins and minerals that work as hard as you do. To fuel your body's powerful energy requirements and replenish your muscle's stores, green veggies are your best bet for complete balanced nutrition!

INGREDIENTS | YIELDS 3–4 CUPS

1 cup collards

1 cup cauliflower

1 cup broccoli

1 carrot, peeled

2 cups purified water

1. Place collards, cauliflower, broccoli, carrot, and 1 cup of water in a blender and blend until thoroughly combined.

2. Add remaining 1 cup of water as needed while blending until desired consistency is achieved.

PER 1 CUP SERVING: Calories: 23 | Fat: 0g | Protein: 1g | Sodium: 30mg | Fiber: 2g | Carbohydrates: 5g

Popeye's Favorite

Popeye had the right idea, and it showed in his powerful abilities.
This recipe is filled with iron, vitamin K, folate, and fiber, and will have you feeling strong like Popeye!

INGREDIENTS | YIELDS 3–4 CUPS

1 cup spinach

1 kale leaf

1 cup broccoli

3 apples, peeled and cored

2 cups purified water

Greens for All

When you were a kid, Popeye was one amazing example of what could happen if you ate your spinach! How many times did your parents reference Popeye when trying to get you to eat your spinach? And how often do you reference strength when trying to get your kids to eat greens now? Spinach is packed with vitamins A, B, C, E, and K as well as iron, phosphorous, and fiber. With all of that nutrition delivered in each serving, spinach should be in every athlete's daily diet . . . for strength like Popeye's!

1. Place spinach, kale, broccoli, apples, and 1 cup of water in a blender and blend until thoroughly combined.

2. Add remaining 1 cup of water as needed while blending until desired consistency is achieved.

PER 1 CUP SERVING: Calories: 76 | Fat: 0g | Protein: 2g | Sodium: 23mg | Fiber: 3g | Carbohydrates: 19g

Metabolism Max Out

Vitamin C plays an important part in fighting illness, promoting your body's ability to function properly in every aspect, and optimizing metabolism for a fat-burning effect like no other.

INGREDIENTS | YIELDS 3–4 CUPS

1 cup watercress

2 cups pineapple, peeled and cored

1 white grapefruit, peeled

3 tangerines, peeled

1 lemon, peeled

1 cup green tea

1. Place watercress, pineapple, grapefruit, tangerines, lemon, and ½ cup tea in a blender and blend until thoroughly combined.

2. Add remaining ½ cup of tea as needed while blending until desired consistency is achieved.

PER 1 CUP SERVING: Calories: 97 | Fat: 0g | Protein: 2g | Sodium: 6mg | Fiber: 2g | Carbohydrates: 25g

Banana Berry Boost

You can't beat the taste of smooth bananas and sweet berries blended with creamy yogurt! There's no better follow-up to a satisfying workout than a dose of sweet fruits blended with powerful protein to optimize your muscles' recovery.

INGREDIENTS | YIELDS 3–4 CUPS

1 cup watercress

2 bananas, peeled

2 cups goji berries

1 cup Greek-style yogurt

The Goji Berry

Goji berries provide excellent benefits for everything from cancer prevention to eye health. Although research has shown the nutrients and phytochemicals in berries are responsible for preventing serious illnesses and diseases, the goji berry's specific effects are still under review. Including these sweet jewels makes a delicious smoothie that will not only satisfy your sweet tooth but also make your body a flu-fighting machine.

1. Place watercress, bananas, goji berries, and ½ cup yogurt in a blender and blend until thoroughly combined.

2. Add remaining ½ cup yogurt as needed while blending until desired consistency is achieved.

PER 1 CUP SERVING: Calories: 266 | Fat: 0g | Protein: 15g | Sodium: 28mg | Fiber: 10g | Carbohydrates: 64g

Vivacious Vitamin C

Eating a balanced diet of vibrant fruits, vegetables, and leafy greens can ensure you're providing for your health and your athletic ability.

INGREDIENTS | YIELDS 3–4 CUPS

1 cup watercress

½ pineapple, peeled and cored

3 oranges, peeled

1 lemon, peeled

1 cup strawberries

1 cup purified water

Vitamins and Minerals for Proactive Health

How important is vitamin C to an athlete? When was the last time you saw a top-performing athlete take first place hacking and heaving all the way to the finish line? Never! If you're going to keep your body in top shape, sound nutrition isn't the only thing requiring attention. In order to get the biggest bang for your buck out of performance nutrition, load up on vibrant fruits and veggies that do double duty.

1. Place watercress, pineapple, oranges, lemon, strawberries, and ½ cup water in a blender and blend until thoroughly combined.

2. Add remaining ½ cup water as needed while blending until desired consistency is achieved.

PER 1 CUP SERVING: Calories: 138 | Fat: 0g | Protein: 3g | Sodium: 7mg | Fiber: 4g | Carbohydrates: 35g

Sweet Potato Smoothie

Even though being an avid athlete means focusing on the healthiest foods that provide ideal nutrition calorie for calorie, cravings for sweet treats creep up every once in a while. Calm those cravings with combinations like this that satisfy with sound nutrition!

INGREDIENTS | YIELDS 3–4 CUPS

½ cup walnuts

2 cups purified water

1 cup spinach

1 sweet potato, peeled and cut for blender's ability

1 teaspoon pumpkin pie spice

1. Combine walnuts and 1 cup of water in a blender and blend until emulsified and no walnut bits remain.

2. Add spinach, sweet potato, pumpkin pie spice, and remaining 1 cup of water while blending until desired consistency is achieved.

PER 1 CUP SERVING: Calories: 127 | Fat: 10g | Protein: 3g | Sodium: 19mg | Fiber: 2g | Carbohydrates: 9g

Walnuts for Athletic Performance

In just ¼ cup of walnuts, you can find almost 100 percent of your daily value of omega-3s with the richness of monounsaturated fats. Not only a tasty, protein-packed morsel, the walnut helps athletes perform at their best by improving circulation and heart health, controlling blood pressure, providing essential amino acids, and acting as a powerful antioxidant.

Cacao Craziness

Chocolate cravings can end in guilty consumption of sugar- and fat-laden candy that leads to the need for more exercise. Satisfy those cravings with pure cacao in a smoothie like this, and candy cravings will be a thing of the past.

INGREDIENTS | YIELDS 3–4 CUPS

¼ cup almonds

2 cups purified water

1 cup watercress

2 tablespoons powdered natural cacao

2 bananas, peeled

2 apples, peeled and cored

1. Combine almonds and 1 cup of water in a blender and emulsify until no almond bits remain.

2. Add watercress, cacao, bananas, apples, and remaining 1 cup of water while blending until desired consistency is achieved.

PER 1 CUP SERVING: Calories: 153 | Fat: 5g | Protein: 3g | Sodium: 7mg | Fiber: 4g | Carbohydrates: 27g

Sweet Antioxidant Protection

When in need of powerful antioxidants that provide and protect, reach no further than a heaping helping of raw cacao. The plant that actually delivers the cocoa we're oh-so-familiar with, cacao is known as a super-food for providing an abundance of antioxidants. Protect your body and the hard work you've put into making it an efficient machine by adding raw cacao in sweet or savory smoothies for an extra bit of health!

Runner's Delight

Any endurance runner feels amped before and pumped following a run. After all that hard work, you're definitely entitled to enjoy a sweet treat. Instead of undoing all that hard work with empty calories, indulge in the sweet taste of citrus with all its added benefits!

INGREDIENTS | YIELDS 3–4 CUPS

1 cup watercress

3 oranges, peeled

1 cup strawberries

1 cup raspberries

1 cup Greek-style yogurt

1. Place watercress, oranges, berries, and ½ cup yogurt in a blender and blend until thoroughly combined.

2. Add remaining ½ cup yogurt as needed while blending until desired consistency is achieved.

PER 1 CUP SERVING: Calories: 126 | Fat: 0g | Protein: 8g | Sodium: 28mg | Fiber: 6g | Carbohydrates: 25g

A Biker's Best Friend

Nothing keeps sustained energy up like slow-releasing carbohydrates. Root vegetables are the best friend of any distance cyclist on a mission for better times and better health!

INGREDIENTS | YIELDS 3–4 CUPS

1 cup spinach

2 yams, peeled

2 apples, peeled and cored

2 carrots, peeled

2 cups purified water

1. Place spinach, yams, apples, carrots, and 1 cup water in a blender and blend until thoroughly combined.

2. Add remaining 1 cup water as needed while blending until desired consistency is achieved.

PER 1 CUP SERVING: Calories: 110 | Fat: 0g | Protein: 2g | Sodium: 50mg | Fiber: 4g | Carbohydrates: 27g

Swimmer's Sensation

Although your time is spent in a body of water, you can come out feeling dehydrated and in need of a boost of energy. A refreshing combination of pineapple, lemon, and cooling cucumbers can deliver exactly what your mind and body need.

INGREDIENTS | YIELDS 3–4 CUPS

1 cup iceberg lettuce

2 cups pineapple, peeled and cored

2 cucumbers, peeled

½ lemon, peeled

1 cup Greek-style yogurt

1. Place iceberg, pineapple, cucumbers, lemon, and ½ cup yogurt in a blender and blend until thoroughly combined.

2. Add remaining ½ cup yogurt as needed while blending until desired consistency is achieved.

PER 1 CUP SERVING: Calories: 86 | Fat: 0g | Protein: 7g | Sodium: 29mg | Fiber: 1g | Carbohydrates: 15g

A Yogi's Favorite

Hot, or not, yoga can be a powerful workout. Replenish your body and refresh your senses with this sweet blend of melons, citrus, and berries. A definite "Yum!" to follow your "Ohm!"

INGREDIENTS | YIELDS 3–4 CUPS

1 cup watercress

½ honeydew, rind and seeds removed

2 tangerines, peeled

1 cucumber, peeled

1 cup Greek-style yogurt

1. Place watercress, honeydew, tangerines, cucumber, and ½ cup yogurt in a blender and blend until thoroughly combined.

2. Add remaining ½ cup yogurt as needed while blending until desired consistency is achieved.

PER 1 CUP SERVING: Calories: 120 | Fat: 0g | Protein: 7g | Sodium: 58mg | Fiber: 2g | Carbohydrates: 24g

Oh, My! Omegas

In this tasty recipe, omega-3s are plentiful without the need for salmon or rich meats.
If salmon isn't your favorite food, consider smoothies that contain flax for your daily value of omegas.

INGREDIENTS | YIELDS 3–4 CUPS

1 cup watercress

½ cantaloupe, rind and seeds removed

1 banana, peeled

1 orange, peeled

1 cup raspberries

1 tablespoon flaxseeds

2 cups purified water

1. Place watercress, cantaloupe, banana, orange, raspberries, flaxseeds, and 1 cup of water in a blender and blend until thoroughly combined.

2. Add remaining 1 cup of water as needed while blending until desired consistency is achieved.

PER 1 CUP SERVING: Calories: 102 | Fat: 2g | Protein: 2g | Sodium: 18mg | Fiber: 5g | Carbohydrates: 23g

Flaxseeds for Omega-3s!

Everybody needs omegas! Although many athletes include meats in their diets, some vegetarian and vegan athletes need to turn to alternatives to fulfill their omega needs. Flaxseeds provide amazing amounts of omegas that are comparable to rich meats and fish (that are also high in undesirable fat content). Flaxseeds make a mildly nutty addition to your favorite smoothie blends.

Fabulous Fructose

*The combination of citrus fruits in this smoothie
will give you the nutrients you need after a great workout.*

INGREDIENTS | YIELDS 3–4 CUPS

1 cup romaine lettuce

½ pineapple, peeled and cored

½ red grapefruit, peeled

1 tangerine, peeled

½ lemon, peeled

½ lime, peeled

1 cup purified water

1. Place romaine, pineapple, grapefruit, tangerine, lemon, lime, and ½ cup water in a blender and blend until thoroughly combined.

2. Add remaining ½ cup water as needed while blending until desired consistency is achieved.

PER 1 CUP SERVING: Calories: 88 | Fat: 0g | Protein: 1g | Sodium: 4mg | Fiber: 2g | Carbohydrates: 23g

Fructose: The Smart Sugar

Fructose, the natural sugar found in fruit, is the healthiest version of sugar because it's an all-natural, nonprocessed version of the table sugars and artificial sweeteners commonly used. As an athlete, fruit is important for the vitamins and minerals and because it can satisfy your cravings for sweets without the unhealthy crash associated with processed sugar or the possible health risks associated with artificial sweeteners.

CHAPTER 12

Smoothies for Pregnancy

Maternity Medley

This delicious smoothie recipe combines sweet fruits and luscious watercress with the zing of ginger to provide an abundance of important vitamins and minerals for your pregnancy. It will also sweeten your day!

INGREDIENTS | YIELDS 3–4 CUPS

1 cup watercress

½ mango, peeled and deseeded

½ pineapple, peeled and cored

2 tangerines, peeled

¼" ginger, peeled

1 cup red raspberry tea

1. Place watercress, mango, pineapple, tangerines, ginger, and ½ cup of tea in a blender and blend until thoroughly combined.

2. Add remaining ½ cup of tea as needed while blending until desired consistency is achieved.

PER 1 CUP SERVING: Calories: 98 | Fat: 0g | Protein: 1g | Sodium: 7mg | Fiber: 1g | Carbohydrates: 25g

Make Calories Count in Pregnancy

Although many women strive for complete nutrition while also appreciating the increase in caloric requirements suggested in pregnancy, some fear excess troublesome weight gain. In order to ensure that your nutrition and your weight gain are ideal for your pregnancy, make every calorie count! Empty-calorie foods like fried foods and sugary treats deliver empty nutrition for your body and your baby, and lead to excessive sodium, sugar, and fat intake, which will result in stubborn post-baby pounds.

Fertility Found!

*A blend of berries, melon, and vanilla downplay the subtle taste
of spinach for a deliciously sweet and tart smoothie that provides vitamins,
minerals, and phytochemicals for better health for mom and baby!*

INGREDIENTS | YIELDS 3–4 CUPS

1 cup spinach

2 cups cranberries

1 cup cantaloupe, rind and seeds removed

Pulp of ½ vanilla bean

1 cup kefir

1. Place spinach, cranberries, cantaloupe, vanilla pulp, and ½ cup kefir in a blender and blend until thoroughly combined.

2. Add remaining ½ cup of kefir as needed while blending until desired consistency is achieved.

PER 1 CUP SERVING: Calories: 78 | Fat: 2g | Protein: 3g | Sodium: 44mg | Fiber: 4g | Carbohydrates: 14g

Copper for Fertility

Alternative and holistic medicine promotes the use of herbs, vitamins, minerals, and herbal teas to remedy infertility in both men and women. Copper enhances iron absorption and reprductive health in the body. Copper is abundant in deep leafy greens, so add more to your diet to increase copper consumption.

Baby, Be Happy

This simple recipe makes a deliciously sweet veggie smoothie you're sure to enjoy. Iron-rich spinach and peas combine with vitamin-rich carrots for a splendid creation that will satisfy your increasing iron needs.

INGREDIENTS | YIELDS 3–4 CUPS

1 cup spinach

1 cup sweet peas

3 carrots, peeled

2 cups red raspberry tea

1. Place spinach, peas, carrots, and 1 cup of tea in a blender and blend until thoroughly combined.

2. Add remaining 1 cup of tea as needed while blending until desired consistency is achieved.

PER 1 CUP SERVING: Calories: 46 | Fat: 0g | Protein: 2g | Sodium: 76mg | Fiber: 3g | Carbohydrates: 9g

Folate for Fine Spines

A sweet blend of fruits and vibrant vegetables makes for one splendid recipe that satisfies a variety of vitamin and mineral requirements.

INGREDIENTS | YIELDS 3–4 CUPS

1 cup spinach

2 carrots, peeled

2 red Gala apples, peeled and cored

1 banana, peeled

2 cups red raspberry tea

1. Place spinach, carrots, apples, banana, and 1 cup of tea in a blender and blend until thoroughly combined.

2. Add remaining 1 cup of tea as needed while blending until desired consistency is achieved.

PER 1 CUP SERVING: Calories: 79 | Fat: 0g | Protein: 1g | Sodium: 30mg | Fiber: 3g | Carbohydrates: 20g

Importance of Folate in Pregnancy

Among the important vitamins and minerals found to prevent birth defects, one of the most well-known is folate. Studies have shown that ideal levels of folate in pregnancy reduce or remedy the chance of neural and spinal-tube defects. You can take a prenatal vitamin that includes folate, but what about natural sources? Eating a diet rich in deep leafy greens and vibrant-green vegetables can provide a great amount of folate naturally.

Veggies for Vitamins

This delicious savory blend of spicy arugula, tomato, onion, cucumber, celery, and garlic combine with natural tea to give your body an amazing amount of vitamins and minerals.

INGREDIENTS | YIELDS 3–4 CUPS

1 cup arugula

1 tomato

1 cucumber, peeled

1 celery stalk

1 green onion

1 garlic clove

2 cups red raspberry tea

1. Place arugula, tomato, cucumber, celery, onion, garlic, and 1 cup of tea in a blender and blend until thoroughly combined.

2. Add remaining 1 cup of tea as needed while blending until desired consistency is achieved.

PER 1 CUP SERVING: Calories: 17 | Fat: 0g | Protein: 1g | Sodium: 15mg | Fiber: 1g | Carbohydrates: 3g

Fabulous Fertility

*This delicious blend of crisp watercress, refreshing melons, and zippy ginger delivers
a taste combination that will refresh your body and mind while satisfying your sweet tooth.*

INGREDIENTS | YIELDS 3–4 CUPS

1 cup watercress

2 cups watermelon, deseeded

½ cantaloupe, rind and seeds removed

½" ginger, peeled

1 cup raspberry red tea leaf tea

Clean Eating for Fertility

Whole health from the inside out is the best place to start when you're trying to conceive. Consuming a diet of fruits and vegetables enables your body to function at optimal efficiency. Start by including bright produce in your daily diet. By providing your body with vibrant nutrition following conception, you're providing your baby with the best chance of survival, health, and immunity.

1. Place watercress, watermelon, cantaloupe, ginger, and ½ cup tea in a blender and blend until thoroughly combined.

2. Add remaining ½ cup of tea as needed while blending until desired consistency is achieved.

PER 1 CUP SERVING: Calories: 38 | Fat: 0g | Protein: 1g | Sodium: 20mg | Fiber: 1g | Carbohydrates: 9g

Luscious Legs in Pregnancy

*One beautiful benefit of this blend is better circulation
and reduced swelling in the legs—bye-bye, cankles!*

INGREDIENTS | YIELDS 3–4 CUPS

1 cup watercress

1 grapefruit, peeled

½ cantaloupe, rind and seeds removed

½ pineapple, peeled and cored

1 cup strawberries

1 cup red raspberry tea

1. Place watercress, grapefruit, cantaloupe, pineapple, strawberries, and ½ cup tea in a blender and blend until thoroughly combined.

2. Add remaining ½ cup tea as needed while blending until desired consistency is achieved.

PER 1 CUP SERVING: Calories: 112 | Fat: 0g | Protein: 2g | Sodium: 17mg | Fiber: 2g | Carbohydrates: 29g

Stomach Soother

*Digestive problems can be easily remedied with smoothies like this one.
The comforting ginger will soothe your stomach while satisfying your taste buds.*

INGREDIENTS | YIELDS 3–4 CUPS

1 cup watercress

3 apples, peeled and cored

1 banana, peeled

½" ginger, peeled

2 cups red raspberry tea

1. Place watercress, apples, banana, ginger, and 1 cup of tea in a blender and blend until thoroughly combined.

2. Add remaining 1 cup of tea as needed while blending until desired consistency is achieved.

PER 1 CUP SERVING: Calories: 86 | Fat: 0g | Protein: 1g | Sodium: 6mg | Fiber: 2g | Carbohydrates: 22g

Morning Sickness Savior

One of the major discomforts of pregnancy can be the queasiness, nausea, and vomiting brought on by almost anything imaginable. This smoothie recipe is perfect for occasional or constant sufferers.

INGREDIENTS | YIELDS 3–4 CUPS

1 cup watercress

1 grapefruit, peeled

½ lemon, peeled

½" ginger, peeled

1 cup red raspberry tea

1. Place watercress, grapefruit, lemon, ginger, and ½ cup tea in a blender and blend until thoroughly combined.

2. Add remaining ½ cup of tea as needed while blending until desired consistency is achieved.

PER 1 CUP SERVING: Calories: 31 | Fat: 0g | Protein: 1g | Sodium: 7mg | Fiber: 1g | Carbohydrates: 8g

Rice Milk for Reproductive Health

This sensational recipe delivers a delightfully creamy smoothie packed with protein, potassium, and omega-3s. It can satisfy your craving for sweets, creaminess, or nutty flavors!

INGREDIENTS | YIELDS 3–4 CUPS

¼ cup almonds

1 tablespoon flaxseeds

2 cups rice milk

1 cup watercress

2 bananas, peeled

1. Combine almonds, flaxseeds, and ½ cup rice milk in a blender and blend until completely emulsified and no bits of almonds remain.

2. Add watercress, bananas, and 1 cup of rice milk and blend until thoroughly combined.

3. Add remaining ½ cup of rice milk as needed while blending until desired consistency is achieved.

PER 1 CUP SERVING: Calories: 149 | Fat: 6g | Protein: 3g | Sodium: 30mg | Fiber: 3g | Carbohydrates: 22g

Peas for a Perfect Pregnancy

Although probably not the veggie that comes to mind when you think "superfood," peas are an excellent source of iron and folate—both important vitamins and minerals for promoting the best health in mom and baby!

INGREDIENTS | YIELDS 3–4 CUPS

1 cup arugula

1 cup sweet peas

2 celery stalks

1 cucumber, peeled

1 cup red raspberry tea

1. Place arugula, sweet peas, celery, cucumber, and ½ cup tea in a blender and blend until thoroughly combined.

2. Add remaining ½ cup of tea as needed while blending until desired consistency is achieved.

PER 1 CUP SERVING: Calories: 36 | Fat: 0g | Protein: 2g | Sodium: 56mg | Fiber: 2g | Carbohydrates: 7g

Berries for Baby

When Mama's happy, everyone's happy. Satisfying and refreshing ingredients combine here for a flavorful smoothie you can enjoy guilt free.

INGREDIENTS | YIELDS 3–4 CUPS

1 cup watercress

2 bananas, peeled

1 cup blueberries

1 cup strawberries

2 cups kefir

1. Place watercress, bananas, berries, and 1 cup kefir in a blender and blend until thoroughly combined.

2. Add remaining 1 cup of kefir as needed while blending until desired consistency is achieved.

PER 1 CUP SERVING: Calories: 167 | Fat: 4g | Protein: 5g | Sodium: 67mg | Fiber: 5g | Carbohydrates: 29g

Refreshing Raspberry Blend

Raspberries offer a tangy taste that is heightened by the sweet pineapple and sour lemon in this recipe. Simple, quick, and delicious, this smoothie will be a favorite go-to when you're in need of a delicious snack in little time.

INGREDIENTS | YIELDS 3–4 CUPS

1 cup watercress
1 cup raspberries
½ pineapple, peeled and cored
½ lemon, peeled
1½ cups kefir

1. Place watercress, raspberries, pineapple, lemon, and ¾ cup of kefir in a blender and blend until thoroughly combined.

2. Add remaining ¾ cup of kefir as needed while blending until desired consistency is achieved.

PER 1 CUP SERVING: Calories: 136 | Fat: 3g | Protein: 4g | Sodium: 52mg | Fiber: 3g | Carbohydrates: 25g

Savory Spinach

The benefits of iron are outstanding, and are even greater in pregnancy. Satisfy nutritional needs and daily requirements with this smoothie recipe that combines the important green leafy veggie with sweet red peppers, vitamin-packed broccoli, and spicy garlic.

INGREDIENTS | YIELDS 3–4 CUPS

1 cup spinach
½ red bell pepper, cored, ribs intact
½ cup broccoli spears
1 garlic clove
2 cups red raspberry tea

1. Place spinach, red pepper, broccoli, garlic, and 1 cup of tea in a blender and blend until thoroughly combined.

2. Add remaining 1 cup of tea as needed while blending until desired consistency is achieved.

PER 1 CUP SERVING: Calories: 15 | Fat: 0g | Protein: 1g | Sodium: 17mg | Fiber: 1g | Carbohydrates: 3g

Very Important Vitamin C

Immunity and health are never as important as when you're pregnant. Caring for your little one starts long before the birth, and building your body's defenses against illness make for a healthier mom and a healthier baby.

INGREDIENTS | YIELDS 3–4 CUPS

1 cup watercress

2 tangerines, peeled

½ grapefruit, peeled

½ pineapple, peeled and cored

½ cantaloupe, rind and seeds removed

1 cup red raspberry tea

1. Place watercress, tangerines, grapefruit, pineapple, and cantaloupe in a blender and blend until thoroughly combined.

2. Add 1 cup of tea as needed while blending until desired consistency is achieved.

PER 1 CUP SERVING: Calories: 114 | Fat: 0g | Protein: 2g | Sodium: 18mg | Fiber: 2g | Carbohydrates: 29g

Vitamin C Double Duty

Not only is vitamin C an important addition to your diet for its strong immunity-building power, this vitamin also benefits the expectant mom by providing optimal brain functioning, which means better mental clarity, improved focus, and an overall feeling of awareness that is far superior to the mental fuzziness commonly referred to as "pregnancy brain."

Imperative Iron

*Skip the chips and go for this savory, satisfying smoothie,
packed with important iron!*

INGREDIENTS | YIELDS 3–4 CUPS

1 cup spinach

2 carrots, peeled

½ cup broccoli spears

½ cup asparagus spears

1 garlic clove

2 cups red raspberry tea

1. Place spinach, carrots, broccoli, asparagus, garlic, and 1 cup of tea in a blender and blend until thoroughly combined.

2. Add remaining 1 cup of tea as needed while blending until desired consistency is achieved.

PER 1 CUP SERVING: Calories: 23 | Fat: 0g | Protein: 1g | Sodium: 34mg | Fiber: 2g | Carbohydrates: 5g

Why Iron Needs Increase in Pregnancy

Pregnant women require 27mg of iron per day (as opposed to 18mg when not pregnant). Because many women are iron deficient prior to becoming pregnant, their needs are even higher and the risks associated with iron deficiencies are more severe. Preterm delivery, low birth weight, and infant mortality are all risks of iron deficiencies in pregnancy. Ensure your body is provided with sufficient nonheme iron—the vitamin C from the broccoli will help improve the absorption of the nonheme iron.

Ginger Melon Stress Meltaway

Although pregnancy is an amazing experience of excitement and anticipation, stress and moodiness can make it unbearable. Calm your nerves while quieting cravings with this delicious combination of watercress, melons, citrus, and ginger.

INGREDIENTS | YIELDS 3–4 CUPS

1 cup watercress

½ cantaloupe, rind and seeds removed

½ honeydew, rind and seeds removed

1 tangerine, peeled

½" ginger, peeled

1 cup red raspberry tea

1. Place watercress, cantaloupe, honeydew, tangerine, and ginger in a blender and blend until thoroughly combined.

2. Add 1 cup of tea as needed while blending until desired consistency is achieved.

PER 1 CUP SERVING: Calories: 94 | Fat: 0g | Protein: 2g | Sodium: 45mg | Fiber: 2g | Carbohydrates: 24g

Candida Cleanser

The discomforts of pregnancy aren't limited to nausea. Bacterial infections resulting from hormonal fluctuations can be worsened with diet and make for an uncomfortable position. Find relief by combating the culprit with smoothies like this one!

INGREDIENTS | YIELDS 3–4 CUPS

1 cup cabbage

½ cup broccoli

½ cup cauliflower

1 celery stalk

2 cups red raspberry tea

1. Place cabbage, broccoli, cauliflower, celery, and 1 cup of tea in a blender and blend until thoroughly combined.

2. Add remaining 1 cup of tea as needed while blending until desired consistency is achieved.

PER 1 CUP SERVING: Calories: 19 | Fat: 0g | Protein: 1g | Sodium: 29mg | Fiber: 2g | Carbohydrates: 4g

Candida Infections

Candida infections result from an overgrowth of the yeast candida, occurring when organisms kill off the protecting beneficial bacteria found in the digestive system. Sufferers experience headaches, bladder infections, indigestion, diarrhea, constipation, and moodiness. Candidia infections can be avoided by changes in diet. Avoiding starchy vegetables like carrots, potatoes, and corn; sugar-laden fruit juices; and implementing a probiotic drink like kefir can starve candida while promoting beneficial bacteria growth.

Illness Preventer

*Protect your body and your baby from illness by packing in the vitamin C.
Not only does this amazing vitamin promote health and immunity,
it can alleviate stress and improve mental stability and happiness.*

INGREDIENTS | YIELDS 3–4 CUPS

1 cup watercress

2 oranges, peeled

½ pineapple, peeled and cored

½ lemon, peeled

½ lime, peeled

1 cup red raspberry tea

1. Place watercress, oranges, pineapple, lemon, and lime in a blender and blend until thoroughly combined.

2. Add 1 cup of tea as needed while blending until desired consistency is achieved.

PER 1 CUP SERVING: Calories: 105 | Fat: 0g | Protein: 2g | Sodium: 6mg | Fiber: 3g | Carbohydrates: 27g

Moodiness Manipulator

Forget all of the nay-sayers who call pregnancy moodiness "crazy."
Forty weeks is a long time, and the hormone fluctuations don't help in maintaining a cool, calm,
and collected composure all the time. Indulge in this delicious treat that will lift your mood!

INGREDIENTS | YIELDS 3–4 CUPS

1 cup watercress
½ cantaloupe, rind and seeds removed
½ lemon, peeled
½" ginger, peeled
1½ cups red raspberry tea

Nutrition for Stability

Creating life requires a lot of energy, and because your growing baby is depending on you for vitamins and minerals, deficiencies can leave you fatigued. Provide your body with all of the necessary vitamins and minerals in amounts that satisfy your needs and your baby's to prevent common symptoms associated with deficiencies. Supplement your pregnancy with a diet rich in leafy greens and vibrant fruits and veggies to improve the amount of vitamins and minerals for mom and baby.

1. Place watercress, cantaloupe, lemon, ginger, and ¾ cup of the tea in a blender and blend until thoroughly combined.

2. Add remaining ¾ cup of tea as needed while blending until desired consistency is achieved.

PER 1 CUP SERVING: Calories: 27 | Fat: 0g | Protein: 1g | Sodium: 17mg | Fiber: 1g | Carbohydrates: 7g

Pleasurable Pregnancy Smoothie

*Pregnancy is an opportunity to give your body the pristine treatment it deserves.
Treat yourself to this delicious smoothie throughout your nine months
and savor the feeling of optimal health!*

INGREDIENTS | YIELDS 3–4 CUPS

1 cup watercress

2 red Gala apples, peeled and cored

1 cup cranberries

¼" ginger, peeled

2 cups red raspberry tea

1. Place watercress, apples, cranberries, ginger, and 1 cup of tea in a blender and blend until thoroughly combined.

2. Add remaining 1 cup of tea as needed while blending until desired consistency is achieved.

PER 1 CUP SERVING: Calories: 51 | Fat: 0g | Protein: 1g | Sodium: 6mg | Fiber: 2g | Carbohydrates: 14g

Pamper Yourself

Whether this is your first pregnancy or the next in a long line of lovable little ones, your pregnancy is a time that requires special attention. The hustle and bustle of everyday life can leave you run down and overwhelmed, but being pregnant can add to exhaustion and lack of focus on yourself. Take the time to spend quiet and quality time on yourself without distraction or stress. Meditation, light exercise, and quality nutrition can be the keys to a pampered pregnancy and provide happiness for all!

CHAPTER 13

Smoothies for Raw-Food Diets

Berry Citrus Banana

The refreshing blend of berries, citrus, and banana combine for a delicious flavor sensation that delivers plentiful antioxidants with a healthy dose of vitamin C.

INGREDIENTS | YIELDS 3–4 CUPS

1 cup romaine lettuce

1 banana, peeled

1 cup strawberries

1 cup blueberries

1 cup blackberries

2 tangerines, peeled

1 cup purified water

1. Place romaine, banana, berries, tangerines, and ½ cup water in a blender and blend until thoroughly combined.

2. Add remaining ½ cup water as needed while blending until desired consistency is achieved.

PER 1 CUP SERVING: Calories: 100 | Fat: 1g | Protein: 2g | Sodium: 4mg | Fiber: 5g | Carbohydrates: 25g

A Natural Thickening Agent?

You can actually watch bananas take a liquefied smoothie and turn it into a delightfully thickened version. Because bananas have such low water content, they can be used as a great natural alternative to common thickening agents. Use bananas as a natural alternative to shelved artificial versions. You can experiment with this smoothie and watch as it thickens the smoothie before your very eyes!

Chocolatey Almond Treat

*Although puréed dates lend a chocolatey sweetness to smoothies
all by themselves, this recipe combines sweet dates, raw cacao powder,
and cayenne pepper for a delightful, slightly spicy chocolate smoothie.*

INGREDIENTS | YIELDS 3–4 CUPS

2 cups purified water

¼ cup almonds

1 cup watercress

1 banana, peeled

2 dates, pitted

1 tablespoon powdered cacao

¼ teaspoon cayenne

Pulp of ½ vanilla bean

1. Combine 1 cup water and almonds in a blender and emulsify until no nut pieces remain.

2. Add watercress, banana, dates, cacao, cayenne, and vanilla bean and blend until thoroughly combined.

3. Add remaining 1 cup of water as needed while blending until desired consistency is achieved.

PER 1 CUP SERVING: Calories: 117 | Fat: 5g | Protein: 3g | Sodium: 7mg | Fiber: 3g | Carbohydrates: 18g

Almond Pear with Cherries

The sweet flavor of almonds gets even sweeter with cherries and pears.
Being healthy and eating healthy by staying away from processed
sugar-packed foods is easy with smoothies like this one!

INGREDIENTS | YIELDS 3–4 CUPS

¼ cup almonds

2 cups purified water

1 cup romaine lettuce

2 pears, cored and peeled

½ cup cherries, pitted

Pulp of ½ vanilla bean

The Power of Copper

A little known fact about the pear is that just one serving contains a powerful amount of copper. A strong and very important mineral, copper works wonders in fighting the process of free radical damage to cells. Not only does this mean a pear can help you fight off cancer and disease, the aesthetic effects of antiaging can be pretty attractive, too!

1. Combine almonds with 1 cup of water in a blender and emulsify until no nut pieces remain.

2. Add romaine, pears, cherries, and vanilla bean and blend until thoroughly combined.

3. Add remaining 1 cup of water as needed while blending until desired consistency is achieved.

PER 1 CUP SERVING: Calories: 117 | Fat: 5g | Protein: 3g | Sodium: 4mg | Fiber: 5g | Carbohydrates: 19g

Citrus Berry Blast

There is nothing more refreshing and uplifting than sweet citrus!
Mind in a fog? Stress levels high? Smoothie combinations like this one
are a delightful remedy to what ails the mind and body!

INGREDIENTS | YIELDS 3–4 CUPS

1 cup watercress

3 oranges, peeled

½ grapefruit, peeled

1 cup strawberries

1 cup blueberries

1 cup purified water

1. Place watercress, oranges, grapefruit, berries, and ½ cup of water in a blender and blend until thoroughly combined.

2. Add remaining ½ cup of water as needed while blending until desired consistency is achieved.

PER 1 CUP SERVING: Calories: 103 | Fat: 0g | Protein: 2g | Sodium: 5mg | Fiber: 5g | Carbohydrates: 26g

Why Grapefruit Is Great

Although the grapefruit is known for being rich in vitamin C, this citrus fruit has not only been used for building immunity, but also for treating symptoms of illness. The next time you start feeling feverish, the best thing to take may just be a healthy helping of grapefruit, which would make this smoothie the perfect option!

Peachy Berries

Providing a wealth of nutrition in every sip, this smoothie makes for a delicious way to meet important fruit and veggie serving requirements with the added benefits of ginger.

INGREDIENTS | YIELDS 3–4 CUPS

1 cup watercress

3 peaches, pitted

1 cup strawberries

1 orange, peeled

¼" ginger, peeled

2 cups purified water

1. Place watercress, peaches, strawberries, orange, and ginger with 1 cup of water in a blender and blend until thoroughly combined.

2. Add remaining 1 cup of water as needed while blending until desired consistency is achieved.

PER 1 CUP SERVING: Calories: 78 | Fat: 0g | Protein: 2g | Sodium: 6mg | Fiber: 4g | Carbohydrates: 19g

Ginger Apple Delight

Delicious fiber-rich apples star in this quick and easy recipe. Romaine provides a crisp background for the sweet apples and smooth banana, and the ginger adds a hint of spice.

INGREDIENTS | YIELDS 3–4 CUPS

1 cup romaine lettuce

2 apples, cored and peeled

1 banana, peeled

¼" ginger, peeled

2 cups purified water

1. Place romaine, apples, banana, ginger, and 1 cup of water in a blender and blend until thoroughly combined.

2. Add remaining 1 cup of water as needed while blending until desired consistency is achieved.

PER 1 CUP SERVING: Calories: 67 | Fat: 0g | Protein: 1g | Sodium: 4mg | Fiber: 2g | Carbohydrates: 17g

Minty Banana Pears

*Sweet pears are made even sweeter by the addition of fresh lemon.
Combined with romaine and deliciously refreshing mint, this unique blend of flavors makes
a wonderfully refreshing treat that will satisfy sweet cravings without added sugar.*

INGREDIENTS | YIELDS 3–4 CUPS

1 cup romaine lettuce

1 tablespoon mint leaves

4 pears, cored and peeled

½ lemon, peeled

2 cups purified water

1. Place romaine, mint, pears, lemon, and 1 cup of water in a blender and blend until thoroughly combined.

2. Add remaining 1 cup of water as needed while blending until desired consistency is achieved.

PER 1 CUP SERVING: Calories: 108 | Fat: 0g | Protein: 1g | Sodium: 6mg | Fiber: 6g | Carbohydrates: 29g

Pineapple Berry

*The important vitamins, minerals, and antioxidants in this smoothie
will provide your body with the boost it needs with a more sustainable
effect than the store-bought, chemically enhanced energy drinks.*

INGREDIENTS | YIELDS 3–4 CUPS

1 cup watercress

2 cups pineapple

1 cup strawberries

1 cup blackberries

1 cup purified water

1. Place watercress, pineapple, strawberries, blackberries, and ½ cup of water in a blender and blend until thoroughly combined.

2. Add remaining ½ cup of water as needed while blending until desired consistency is achieved.

PER 1 CUP SERVING: Calories: 65 | Fat: 0g | Protein: 1g | Sodium: 6mg | Fiber: 3g | Carbohydrates: 16g

Apricot-Banana Wonder

Sweet fruits make for delicious smoothies, and bananas act as a natural thickening agent as opposed to lactose-packed milk alternatives.

INGREDIENTS | YIELDS 3–4 CUPS

1 cup romaine lettuce
3 apricots
2 bananas, peeled
¼" ginger, peeled
2 cups purified water

1. Place romaine, apricots, bananas, ginger, and 1 cup of water in a blender and blend until thoroughly combined.

2. Add remaining 1 cup of water as needed while blending until desired consistency is achieved.

PER 1 CUP SERVING: Calories: 68 | Fat: 0g | Protein: 1g | Sodium: 4mg | Fiber: 2g | Carbohydrates: 17g

Coco-Nana

Coconuts and bananas are an exciting pair in this recipe! The tropical flavors of the coconut with a hint of cinnamon are a wonderful treat for the morning or as a delicious dessert.

INGREDIENTS | YIELDS 3–4 CUPS

1 cup watercress

Flesh of ½ coconut

2 bananas, peeled

¼ teaspoon cinnamon

2 cups purified water

1. Place watercress, coconut flesh, bananas, cinnamon, and 1 cup of water in a blender and blend until thoroughly combined.

2. Add remaining 1 cup of water as needed while blending until desired consistency is achieved.

PER 1 CUP SERVING: Calories: 230 | Fat: 17g | Protein: 2g | Sodium: 15mg | Fiber: 6g | Carbohydrates: 21g

Ginger Citrus

The tang of sweet citrus and the zing of ginger make a stimulating blend that will get your senses and taste buds on high alert. Delicious and rejuvenating, any stressful day can be turned around in no time by indulging in this treat!

INGREDIENTS | YIELDS 3–4 CUPS

1 cup watercress

2 cups pineapple, peeled and cored

2 bananas, peeled

¼" ginger, peeled

1 cup purified water

1. Place watercress, pineapple, bananas, ginger, and ½ cup water in a blender and blend until thoroughly combined.

2. Add remaining ½ cup of water as needed while blending until desired consistency is achieved.

PER 1 CUP SERVING: Calories: 91 | Fat: 0g | Protein: 1g | Sodium: 6mg | Fiber: 2g | Carbohydrates: 23g

Feed Your Brain

With 4 servings of fruit and 2 servings of vegetables in this smoothie, the vitamin and mineral benefits are obvious, but this citrusy green mix is especially high in iron and folate. Necessary for optimal brain functioning, folate is especially important for pregnant and nursing women.

Green Tea Green Smoothie

*With all of the intense nutrition packed into a green smoothie,
how could it get any better? Add powerful antioxidant-rich green tea
to the vitamins and minerals provided by the rich greens and citrus!*

INGREDIENTS | YIELDS 3–4 CUPS

1 cup spinach

2 lemons, peeled

½" ginger, peeled

1 tablespoon raw honey

2 cups green tea

1. Place spinach, lemons, ginger, honey, and 1 cup of tea in a blender and blend until thoroughly combined.

2. Add remaining 1 cup of tea as needed while blending until desired consistency is achieved.

PER 1 CUP SERVING: Calories: 37 | Fat: 0g | Protein: 1g | Sodium: 9mg | Fiber: 1g | Carbohydrates: 10g

Orange-Mango Tango

*Beta-carotene-rich fruits add much-needed health benefits
to this vitamin-packed green smoothie.*

INGREDIENTS | YIELDS 3–4 CUPS

1 cup watercress
2 cups mango, peeled and pitted
2 oranges, peeled
¼" ginger, peeled (optional)
2 cups purified water

1. Place watercress, mango, oranges, ginger, and 1 cup water in a blender and blend until thoroughly combined.

2. Add remaining 1 cup of water as needed while blending until desired consistency is achieved.

PER 1 CUP SERVING: Calories: 98 | Fat: 0g | Protein: 1g | Sodium: 8mg | Fiber: 4g | Carbohydrates: 25g

Spicy Cocoa

*This recipe takes sweet and spicy to the next level by providing
the flavorful combination of sweet chocolate and hot pepper with the
added health benefits found in every ingredient.*

INGREDIENTS | YIELDS 3–4 CUPS

1 cup spinach
2 bananas, peeled
1 tablespoon powdered cacao
1 tablespoon raw honey
1 teaspoon cinnamon
⅛ teaspoon cayenne
2 cups almond milk

1. Place spinach, bananas, cacao, honey, cinnamon, cayenne, and 1 cup almond milk in a blender and blend until thoroughly combined.

2. Add remaining 1 cup of almond milk as needed while blending until desired consistency is achieved.

PER 1 CUP SERVING: Calories: 121 | Fat: 2g | Protein: 2g | Sodium: 82mg | Fiber: 3g | Carbohydrates: 27g

Kiwi-Mango Combo

Tropical kiwifruit takes a star presence in this deliciously sweet treat that will provide tons of fruit servings without weighing you down.

INGREDIENTS | YIELDS 3–4 CUPS

1 cup watercress

2 cups mango, peeled and pitted

2 tangerines, peeled

4 kiwifruit, peeled

½ lemon, peeled

2 cups purified water

1. Place watercress, mango, tangerines, kiwi, lemon, and 1 cup of water in a blender and blend until thoroughly combined.

2. Add remaining 1 cup of water as needed while blending until desired consistency is achieved.

PER 1 CUP SERVING: Calories: 126 | Fat: 1g | Protein: 2g | Sodium: 11mg | Fiber: 5g | Carbohydrates: 32g

Mangoes and Complexion

If you suffer from any type of skin abnormalities such as rashes, eczema, or even clogged pores, mangoes contain strong minerals, phytochemicals, and phenols that can improve the condition of your skin. The sweet taste of a mango smoothie with the added benefit of clear skin is a definite win-win!

Cherry-Banana Bliss

This delicious, thick fruit blend also has a mild sweet nuttiness from the almond milk.
This is a filling smoothie with no guilt and tons of flavor.

INGREDIENTS | YIELDS 3–4 CUPS

1 cup spinach
2 cups cherries, pitted
2 bananas, peeled
½ lemon, peeled
2 cups almond milk

1. Place spinach, cherries, bananas, lemon, and 1 cup of almond milk in a blender and blend until thoroughly combined.

2. Add remaining 1 cup of almond milk as needed while blending until desired consistency is achieved.

PER 1 CUP SERVING: Calories: 150 | Fat: 2g | Protein: 2g | Sodium: 82mg | Fiber: 4g | Carbohydrates: 35g

Pomegranate and Protein

*Adding raw hemp seed protein powder to any of your favorite green smoothies
is a delicious way to increase your protein intake.*

INGREDIENTS | YIELDS 3–4 CUPS

1 cup spinach

4 tablespoons raw hemp seed protein
powder

Pips of 2 pomegranates

1 cup strawberries

1 cup raspberries

1 banana, peeled

2 cups almond milk

1. Place spinach, hemp protein, pomegranate pips, berries, banana, and 1 cup almond milk in a blender and blend until thoroughly combined.

2. Add remaining 1 cup of almond milk as needed while blending until desired consistency is achieved.

PER 1 CUP SERVING: Calories: 225 | Fat: 4g | Protein: 8g | Sodium: 52mg | Fiber: 11g | Carbohydrates: 46g

Nuts and Berries

Sounding like a true tree-hugger's dream smoothie, this recipe appeals to anyone in search of better health from the best nutrition. The omega-3 content of this smoothie comes from the smart addition of flaxseeds, which also adds even more nutty flavor.

INGREDIENTS | YIELDS 3–4 CUPS

2 cups almond milk

¼ cup almonds

1 tablespoon flaxseeds

1 cup spinach

2 cups strawberries

3 rhubarb stalks

1. Combine 1 cup almond milk with the almonds and flaxseeds in a blender and emulsify completely until no nut pieces remain.

2. Add spinach, strawberries, and rhubarb and blend until thoroughly combined.

3. Add remaining 1 cup of almond milk as needed while blending until desired consistency is achieved.

PER 1 CUP SERVING: Calories: 131 | Fat: 7g | Protein: 4g | Sodium: 84mg | Fiber: 4g | Carbohydrates: 15g

Sweet Veggie Surprise

With this smoothie, you can savor the delicious flavor of red peppers, vibrant beets, lycopene-rich tomatoes, beta-carotene-packed carrots, and spicy cilantro.

INGREDIENTS | YIELDS 3–4 CUPS

1 cup spinach

1 tomato

4 carrots, peeled

1 beet, greens removed

½ red bell pepper, cored with ribs intact

⅛ cup cilantro

2½ cups purified water

1. Place spinach, tomato, carrots, beet, red pepper, cilantro, and 1¼ cups of water in a blender and blend until thoroughly combined.

2. Add remaining 1¼ cup of the water as needed while blending until desired consistency is achieved.

PER 1 CUP SERVING: Calories: 46 | Fat: 0g | Protein: 2g | Sodium: 69mg | Fiber: 3g | Carbohydrates: 10g

Carrots Can Save the Day!

This vegetable is a must have in your daily diet! Its rich orange color is the tell-tale sign that it is rich in beta-carotene (vitamin A), but it's also packed with B vitamins, biotin, vitamin K, and potassium. Perfect in sweet or savory smoothies, this veggie makes a great addition or star ingredient. Talk about a multitasker perfect in any raw-food diet!

Herbal Peach

Green tea is the ingredient responsible for loading antioxidants into this flavorful smoothie! It's easy to combat illnesses and promote health and wellness for your body and mind with this quick and easy recipe.

INGREDIENTS | YIELDS 2–3 CUPS

1 cup spinach

⅛ cup parsley

2 peaches, pitted

½ lemon, peeled

2 cups green tea

1. Place spinach, parsley, peaches, lemon, and 1 cup of tea in a blender and blend until thoroughly combined.

2. Add remaining 1 cup of tea as needed while blending until desired consistency is achieved.

PER 1 CUP SERVING: Calories: 35 | Fat: 0g | Protein: 1g | Sodium: 7mg | Fiber: 2g | Carbohydrates: 9g

Green Tea's Power

The importance of herbal tea can be seen in its use in Eastern medicinal culture. Used as a remedy for many illnesses and to promote natural health, green tea's amazing health benefits come from its rich concentration of powerful antioxidants. Antioxidants combat serious illnesses and disease and cleanse the body of toxins and waste, all while providing improved immunity, optimal functioning of the body's processes, and a great-tasting substitute to water.

Papaya Protein

The delicious flavors of papaya, banana, date, vanilla, and sweet almond milk virtually dance on your tongue while satisfying your body's needs and your cravings for sweets.

INGREDIENTS | YIELDS 3–4 CUPS

1 cup watercress

2 cups papaya

1 banana, peeled

1 date, pitted

Pulp of 1 vanilla bean

1 tablespoon raw hemp seed protein

2 cups almond milk

1. Place watercress, papaya, banana, date, vanilla bean pulp, hemp protein, and 1 cup almond milk in a blender and blend until thoroughly combined.

2. Add remaining 1 cup of almond milk as needed while blending until desired consistency is achieved.

PER 1 CUP SERVING: Calories: 124 | Fat: 2g | Protein: 2g | Sodium: 82mg | Fiber: 3g | Carbohydrates: 27g

CHAPTER 14

Antiaging and Body Care Smoothies

Spicy Refreshment

Spicy arugula gets sweetened up a bit with pears, grapes, and zippy ginger to make a wonderful smoothie. This recipe is full of vitamins, minerals, and antioxidants that provide total health, beautiful eyes, and luxurious skin.

INGREDIENTS | YIELDS 3–4 CUPS

1 cup arugula

4 pears, peeled and cored

1 cup red grapes

½" ginger, peeled

2 cups chamomile tea

1. Place arugula, pears, grapes, ginger, and 1 cup of tea in a blender and blend until thoroughly combined.

2. Add remaining 1 cup of tea as needed while blending until desired consistency is achieved.

PER 1 CUP SERVING: Calories: 131 | Fat: 0g | Protein: 1g | Sodium: 23mg | Fiber: 6g | Carbohydrates: 35g

Balanced Diet for Better Skin

Crash dieting is a definite no-no when trying to clear up acne! Studies have shown that extreme changes in diet like the total avoidance of fats or excessive inclusion of fats as the sole source of food can destabilize the amount of secretions of the pores, which is the major source of acne. So, include a variety of fresh fruits and veggies with little fats to promote the most balanced environment for beautiful skin!

Bone Up with Blackberries

Rich vitamins and minerals that will optimize all those steps you take for health are abundant in this smoothie recipe.

INGREDIENTS | YIELDS 3–4 CUPS

1 cup watercress

2 cups blackberries

2 bananas, peeled

2 oranges, peeled

2 cups chamomile tea

1. Place watercress, blackberries, bananas, oranges, and 1 cup tea in a blender and blend until thoroughly combined.

2. Add remaining 1 cup of tea as needed while blending until desired consistency is achieved.

PER 1 CUP SERVING: Calories: 128 | Fat: 1g | Protein: 3g | Sodium: 7mg | Fiber: 8g | Carbohydrates: 32g

Backwards Berry

*Beautiful, healthier, more hydrated skin and hair are added
benefits from this smoothie. The antioxidants provided protect against
free radical damage that can wreak havoc on the inside and outside of your body.*

INGREDIENTS | YIELDS 3–4 CUPS

1 cup spinach
1 pint blackberries
1 pint raspberries
¼" ginger, peeled
½ lemon, peeled
2 cups chamomile tea

1. Place spinach, berries, ginger, lemon, and 1 cup of tea in a blender and blend until thoroughly combined.

2. Add remaining 1 cup of tea as needed while blending until desired consistency is achieved.

PER 1 CUP SERVING: Calories: 67 | Fat: 1g | Protein: 2g | Sodium: 10mg | Fiber: 8g | Carbohydrates: 16g

Double-Duty Delight

Luscious fruits like papaya, pineapple, and strawberries make a perfect blend with delicious vitamin- and mineral-rich romaine. This smoothie's powerful antioxidants will make you look and feel younger.

INGREDIENTS | YIELDS 3–4 CUPS

1 cup romaine lettuce

1 cup papaya

1 cup pineapple, peeled and cubed

1 pint strawberries

2 cups chamomile tea

1. Place romaine, papaya, pineapple, strawberries, and 1 cup tea in a blender and blend until thoroughly combined.

2. Add remaining 1 cup of tea as needed while blending until desired consistency is achieved.

PER 1 CUP SERVING: Calories: 46 | Fat: 0g | Protein: 1g | Sodium: 5mg | Fiber: 2g | Carbohydrates: 11g

GrAppleBerry

Morning, noon, or night, you can enjoy this delightful treat packed with powerful nutrition. Promoting total health on the inside and out, this recipe provides balanced nutrition for any and all health issues.

INGREDIENTS | YIELDS 3–4 CUPS

1 cup watercress

1 cup red grapes

2 apples, peeled and cored

1 pint raspberries

2 cups chamomile tea

1. Place watercress, grapes, apples, raspberries, and 1 cup of tea in a blender and blend until thoroughly combined.

2. Add remaining 1 cup of tea as needed while blending until desired consistency is achieved.

PER 1 CUP SERVING: Calories: 98 | Fat: 1g | Protein: 1g | Sodium: 7mg | Fiber: 5g | Carbohydrates: 25g

Strawberries for Disease Prevention

Strawberries are a delicious, sweet treat, and they're amazingly healthy, too. Packed with B vitamins, vitamin C, and ellagic acid (an anticancer compound), these rich berries prevent disease and cancer. Shown to help reduce the risk of Alzheimer's disease and lower bad cholesterol, strawberries are essential for any diet in need of an extra boost.

Sunburn Soother

*It's funny to think you could soothe a sunburn with a sweet green smoothie,
but it can be done! The hydrating melons are responsible for not only calming skin discomfort,
but also provide electrolytes that promote balance for the body and the mind.*

INGREDIENTS | YIELDS 3–4 CUPS

1 cup arugula

2 cups watermelon, deseeded

2 cups cantaloupe, rind and seeds removed

½ lemon, peeled

½ lime, peeled

½" ginger, peeled

2 cups chamomile tea

1. Place arugula, watermelon, cantaloupe, lemon, lime, ginger, and 1 cup of tea in a blender and blend until thoroughly combined.

2. Add remaining 1 cup of tea as needed while blending until desired consistency is achieved.

PER 1 CUP SERVING: Calories: 56 | Fat: 0g | Protein: 1g | Sodium: 17mg | Fiber: 2g | Carbohydrates: 15g

Melons for Disease Protection

Although most people enjoy these fruits for their hydrating qualities and deliciously sweet flavor, watermelons and cantaloupes are strong warriors in the fight against cancer. Enhancing the immune system with their wealth in B vitamins and vitamin C, these melons have shown to reduce the risks of certain cancers including prostate, ovarian, cervical, oral, and pharyngeal cancers.

Agent Pineapple Against Arthritis

This vitamin-packed smoothie does a world of good for preventing discomfort associated with everything from common colds to arthritis. Sweet, satisfying, and full of fruits and veggies, this is one smoothie that does it all!

INGREDIENTS | YIELDS 3–4 CUPS

1 cup watercress

1 pint blueberries

2 cups pineapple, peeled and cored

¼" ginger, peeled

2 cups chamomile tea

1. Place watercress, blueberries, pineapple, ginger, and 1 cup of tea in a blender and blend until thoroughly combined.

2. Add remaining 1 cup of tea as needed while blending until desired consistency is achieved.

PER 1 CUP SERVING: Calories: 81 | Fat: 0g | Protein: 1g | Sodium: 7mg | Fiber: 2g | Carbohydrates: 21g

Pineapple Prevention

Did you know that every bite of pineapple has powerful protecting vitamins and enzymes that can drastically reduce the discomfort associated with common ailments? The vitamin C content and the enzyme bromelain are responsible for the major health benefits offered up by this super fruit. Those suffering from asthma, arthritis, angina, and indigestion can find extra relief from indulging in one of nature's most delightfully sweet treats.

Fat-Burning Fuel

*The refreshing combination of watermelon, raspberries, lime,
crisp romaine, and calming chamomile will take your life to new heights
by improving metabolism and promoting healthy brain function.*

INGREDIENTS | YIELDS 3–4 CUPS

1 cup romaine lettuce

2 cups watermelon, deseeded

1 pint raspberries

½ lime, peeled

1 cup chamomile tea

1. Place romaine, watermelon, raspberries, lime, and ½ cup of tea in a blender and blend until thoroughly combined.

2. Add remaining ½ cup of tea as needed while blending until desired consistency is achieved.

PER 1 CUP SERVING: Calories: 59 | Fat: 1g | Protein: 1g | Sodium: 4mg | Fiber: 5g | Carbohydrates: 14g

Ache Aid

Reducing aches, pains, soreness, and stiffness can be as easy as blending this delicious fruit, veggie, and herb smoothie that will get you up and moving again!

INGREDIENTS | YIELDS 3–4 CUPS

1 cup watercress

2 cups cantaloupe, rind and seeds removed

1 cucumber, peeled

2 tablespoons mint leaves

¼" ginger, peeled

1 cup chamomile tea

1. Place watercress, cantaloupe, cucumber, mint, ginger, and ½ cup tea in a blender and blend until thoroughly combined.

2. Add remaining ½ cup of tea as needed while blending until desired consistency is achieved.

PER 1 CUP SERVING: Calories: 35 | Fat: 0g | Protein: 1g | Sodium: 19mg | Fiber: 1g | Carbohydrates: 8g

Bright Fight Against Disease

It's well known that fruits and veggies signal their potency with their vibrant colors, so imagine the powerful nutrition and antioxidant power of this delightful blend! Mangoes, strawberries, lemon, sweet romaine, and soothing chamomile combine to fight illness.

INGREDIENTS | YIELDS 3–4 CUPS

1 cup romaine lettuce

2 cups mangoes

1 pint strawberries

½ lemon, peeled

2 cups chamomile tea

Food Combining for Optimal Benefits

When you're looking for the benefits from fruits and vegetables, how can you possibly decide which is the best? With the varied vitamin and mineral contents in different fruits and vegetables, there's no one "best." Your best bet would be to include as much nutrition from fruits and vegetables in as wide a variety as possible; the benefits to your immune system, major bodily functions, brain chemistry, and mental processes are innumerable!

1. Place romaine, mangoes, strawberries, lemon, and 1 cup of tea in a blender and blend until thoroughly combined.

2. Add remaining 1 cup of tea as needed while blending until desired consistency is achieved.

PER 1 CUP SERVING: Calories: 81 | Fat: 0g | Protein: 1g | Sodium: 6mg | Fiber: 3g | Carbohydrates: 21g

Smart Start

This smoothie is the perfect way to start your day! Loaded with vitamin- and mineral-rich fruits and greens, this recipe's nutrition and sustaining benefits will last throughout your day.

INGREDIENTS | YIELDS 4–6 CUPS

1 cup spinach
2 apples, peeled and cored
2 pears, peeled and cored
2 bananas, peeled
¼" ginger, peeled
2 cups chamomile tea

1. Place spinach, apples, pears, bananas, ginger, and 1 cup of tea in a blender and blend until thoroughly combined.

2. Add remaining 1 cup of tea as needed while blending until desired consistency is achieved.

PER 1 CUP SERVING: Calories: 8 | Fat: 0g | Protein: 1g | Sodium: 6mg | Fiber: 3g | Carbohydrates: 22g

Very Green Smoothie

*This very green smoothie combines a variety of greens for the
very best benefits! Spinach, kale, and wheatgrass are packed with vitamins and
minerals that work hard to maintain your health.*

INGREDIENTS | YIELDS 3–4 CUPS

1 cup spinach

2 kale leaves

1 cup wheatgrass

1 celery stalk

½ lemon, peeled

1 garlic clove

2 cups chamomile tea

1. Place spinach, kale, wheatgrass, celery, lemon, garlic, and 1 cup of tea in a blender and blend until thoroughly combined.

2. Add remaining 1 cup of tea as needed while blending until desired consistency is achieved.

PER 1 CUP SERVING: Calories: 16 | Fat: 0g | Protein: 1g | Sodium: 25mg | Fiber: 1g | Carbohydrates: 3g

Root Veggie Variety

Root vegetables are packed with especially high levels of minerals
that promote eye health and offer protection against a number of cancers.
Drink up to promote the best defense against serious illnesses.

INGREDIENTS | YIELDS 3–4 CUPS

1 cup romaine lettuce

1 turnip, peeled and cut to blender capacity

3 carrots, peeled

1 apple, peeled and cored

2 cups purified water

1. Place romaine, turnip, carrots, apple, and 1 cup of water in a blender and blend until thoroughly combined.

2. Add remaining 1 cup of water as needed while blending until desired consistency is achieved.

PER 1 CUP SERVING: Calories: 49 | Fat: 0g | Protein: 1g | Sodium: 55mg | Fiber: 3g | Carbohydrates: 12g

Maximize Your Root Veggie's Potential

One of the many reasons raw-food enthusiasts adopt and adhere to the raw-food diet is the dramatic drop in vitamins, minerals, and nutrients when produce is heated above a certain temperature. Most people prefer to have their root vegetables steamed, mashed, baked, or roasted, which may taste great, but the scorching heat also scorches a large percentage of the nutrient content. Blending these veggies in a green smoothie is a delicious way to enjoy these superfoods with all of the nutrition nature intended.

Memory Maintainer

Protecting your brain was never this delicious! The vitamins, minerals, and antioxidants that promote optimal functioning of your mental processes also prevent the brain's deterioration from illness and disease. This is one smoothie you won't forget!

INGREDIENTS | YIELDS 3–4 CUPS

1 cup romaine lettuce

½ cup broccoli

½ cup cauliflower

1 tomato

1 garlic clove

2 cups purified water

1. Place romaine, broccoli, cauliflower, tomato, garlic, and 1 cup of water in a blender and blend until thoroughly combined.

2. Add remaining 1 cup of water as needed while blending until desired consistency is achieved.

PER 1 CUP SERVING: Calories: 16 | Fat: 0g | Protein: 1g | Sodium: 12mg | Fiber: 1g | Carbohydrates: 3g

Colorful Combo for Cancer Prevention

Combining for a sweet, down-to-earth flavor, the fruits and vegetables with dark leafy greens and chamomile make an intoxicating blend for your mind and body's total health.

INGREDIENTS | YIELDS 3–4 CUPS

1 cup romaine lettuce

2 cups cantaloupe, rind and seeds removed

2 carrots, peeled

1 cup pineapple

1 beet

2 cups chamomile tea

1. Place romaine, cantaloupe, carrots, pineapple, beet, and 1 cup of tea in a blender and blend until thoroughly combined.

2. Add remaining 1 cup of tea as needed while blending until desired consistency is achieved.

PER 1 CUP SERVING: Calories: 68 | Fat: 0g | Protein: 2g | Sodium: 53mg | Fiber: 2g | Carbohydrates: 17g

Mental Makeover

*Hate forgetting things? Feel like you have absentmindedness a little too often?
This smoothie is designed to get your brain back on track with rich sources of vitamins
and minerals that stimulate and rejuvenate brain functions.*

INGREDIENTS | YIELDS 3–4 CUPS

1 cup spinach

2 cucumbers, peeled

2 celery stalks

1 tomato

2 cups chamomile tea

1. Place spinach, cucumbers, celery, tomato, and 1 cup of tea in a blender and blend until thoroughly combined.

2. Add remaining 1 cup of tea as needed while blending until desired consistency is achieved.

PER 1 CUP SERVING: Calories: 25 | Fat: 0g | Protein: 1g | Sodium: 29mg | Fiber: 2g | Carbohydrates: 5g

The Many Hats of Spinach

In addition to being a rich source of iron and folate (which actually aids in iron absorption), this amazing veggie holds a wealth of vitamins A, B, C, D, and K that provide cancer-fighting power against liver, ovarian, colon, and prostate cancers. By including just 1 cup of this powerful veggie in your daily diet (raw), you can satisfy over 180 percent of your daily value for vitamin K and almost 400 percent of your vitamin A intake!

Savor Cancer Prevention

Protect yourself by arming your body's defenses with great nutrition that will not only create energy, focus, and total health, but is a strong prevention against cancers, too.

INGREDIENTS | YIELDS 3–4 CUPS

½ cup romaine lettuce

½ cup spinach

½ cup broccoli

½ cup cauliflower

2 carrots, peeled

1 celery stalk

1 garlic clove

2 cups chamomile tea

1. Place romaine, spinach, broccoli, cauliflower, carrots, celery, garlic, and 1 cup of tea in a blender and blend until thoroughly combined.

2. Add remaining 1 cup of tea as needed while blending until desired consistency is achieved.

PER 1 CUP SERVING: Calories: 24 | Fat: 0g | Protein: 1g | Sodium: 42mg | Fiber: 2g | Carbohydrates: 5g

Red Bells Make Hearts Ring

Delicious red peppers star in this simple savory smoothie. Packed with aromatic red bell peppers, spicy arugula, cooling cucumbers, and crisp celery, this combination is perfect for a filling meal that tastes great and makes for a strong heart.

INGREDIENTS | YIELDS 3–4 CUPS

1 cup arugula

1 red bell pepper, top removed and ribs intact

2 cucumbers, peeled

2 celery stalks

2 cups chamomile tea

1. Place arugula, red pepper, cucumbers, celery, and 1 cup of tea in a blender and blend until thoroughly combined.

2. Add remaining 1 cup of tea as needed while blending until desired consistency is achieved.

PER 1 CUP SERVING: Calories: 26 | Fat: 0g | Protein: 1g | Sodium: 23mg | Fiber: 2g | Carbohydrates: 5g

Antioxidant Assist

No matter how healthy your body may feel, there's always room for some assistance by antioxidants. Warding off illness and preventing degeneration of your body's processes is the main responsibility of these powerful preventers.

INGREDIENTS | YIELDS 3–4 CUPS

½ cup arugula

½ cup spinach

½ cup asparagus

½ cup broccoli

1 clove garlic

2 cups chamomile tea

1. Place arugula, spinach, asparagus, broccoli, garlic, and 1 cup of tea in a blender and blend until thoroughly combined.

2. Add remaining 1 cup of tea as needed while blending until desired consistency is achieved.

PER 1 CUP SERVING: Calories: 13 | Fat: 0g | Protein: 1g | Sodium: 14mg | Fiber: 1g | Carbohydrates: 3g

Carotenes Against Cancer

*The potent healing powers of beta-carotenes are unleashed in this
delicious blend of carrots and sweet potatoes. A satisfying treat for any sweet tooth,
you'll be protecting your health with each delicious sip!*

INGREDIENTS | YIELDS 3–4 CUPS

1 cup romaine lettuce

3 carrots, peeled

1 cup sweet potato

¼" ginger, peeled

2 cups chamomile tea

1. Place romaine, carrots, sweet potato, ginger, and 1 cup of tea in a blender and blend until thoroughly combined.

2. Add remaining 1 cup of tea as needed while blending until desired consistency is achieved.

PER 1 CUP SERVING: Calories: 50 | Fat: 0g | Protein: 1g | Sodium: 53mg | Fiber: 3g | Carbohydrates: 12g

Cauliflower to the Rescue

*This sweet veggie makes a grand entrance for brain and heart health. Including this
powerful veggie in this delicious smoothie makes a great recipe even greater!*

INGREDIENTS | YIELDS 3–4 CUPS

1 cup romaine lettuce

1 cup cauliflower

2 carrots, peeled

1 apple, peeled and cored

2 cups chamomile

1. Place romaine, cauliflower, carrots, apple, and 1 cup of tea in a blender and blend until thoroughly combined.

2. Add remaining cup of tea as needed while blending until desired consistency is achieved.

PER 1 CUP SERVING: Calories: 40 | Fat: 0g | Protein: 1g | Sodium: 32mg | Fiber: 2g | Carbohydrates: 10g

Ever Heard of Allicin?

Packed with important nutrition that satisfies daily dietary needs, this stark white veggie has a powerful secret weapon, too. Cauliflower provides allicin, an important compound that actually reduces the risk of stroke and heart disease while detoxifying the blood and liver. With abilities like that, this veggie is a must have in any disease-preventing diet.

CHAPTER 15

Smoothies for Digestive Health

Indigestion Inhibitor

Digestion discomfort can be painful, and the resulting gassy symptoms can be downright embarrassing. This delightful blend of sweet fruits and veggies combines with chamomile tea for a wonderful soothing effect on indigestion.

INGREDIENTS | YIELDS 3–4 CUPS

1 cup watercress

1 carrot, peeled

1 apple, peeled and cored

1 pear, peeled and cored

¼" ginger, peeled

2 cups chamomile tea

1. Place watercress, carrot, apple, pear, ginger, and 1 cup of tea in a blender and blend until thoroughly combined.

2. Add remaining 1 cup of tea as needed while blending until desired consistency is achieved.

PER 1 CUP SERVING: Calories: 53 | Fat: 0g | Protein: 1g | Sodium: 15mg | Fiber: 2g | Carbohydrates: 14g

Why Fruits and Vegetables Aid Digestion

Research shows that diets high in fiber and complex carbohydrates, both found in abundance in fruits and vegetables, promote healthy digestive systems and can reduce many digestive disorders. Indigestion, ulcers, low stomach acid, constipation, diarrhea, motion sickness, colitis, and many more can be relieved or reversed with the power of produce.

Perfect Pears and Pineapples

The amazing flavors of pineapples and pears are enhanced by the addition of lemon in this recipe. With strong vitamins and minerals that act to aid in digestion and prevent discomfort, this is a splendid blend for any indigestion sufferer.

INGREDIENTS | YIELDS 3–4 CUPS

1 cup romaine lettuce

2 cups pineapple

2 pears, peeled and cored

1 lemon, peeled

2 cups chamomile tea

1. Place romaine, pineapple, pears, lemon, and 1 cup of tea in a blender and blend until thoroughly combined.

2. Add remaining 1 cup of tea as needed while blending until desired consistency is achieved.

PER 1 CUP SERVING: Calories: 95 | Fat: 0g | Protein: 1g | Sodium: 5mg | Fiber: 3g | Carbohydrates: 25g

Amazing Apples for Digestion

Apples star in this delightful recipe because of their high fiber content. With the added benefits from pineapple's vitamin C stores, this combination of deep greens, vibrant fruits, and chamomile tea will make your digestive system perform at peak functioning!

INGREDIENTS | YIELDS 3–4 CUPS

1 cup watercress

3 apples, peeled and cored

1 cup pineapple

¼" ginger, peeled

2 cups chamomile tea

1. Place watercress, apples, pineapple, ginger, and 1 cup of tea in a blender and blend until thoroughly combined.

2. Add remaining 1 cup of tea as needed while blending until desired consistency is achieved.

PER 1 CUP SERVING: Calories: 78 | Fat: 0g | Protein: 1g | Sodium: 6mg | Fiber: 2g | Carbohydrates: 20g

Dreamy Digestion

On the uncomfortable nights that indigestion creeps up, turn to your blender for quick relief. This delightfully sweet fruit and veggie combination provides indigestion relief in one treat you can enjoy as dessert or right when the burn hits!

INGREDIENTS | YIELDS 3–4 CUPS

1 cup romaine lettuce

2 apples, cored and peeled

2 carrots, peeled

1 cucumber, peeled

½ lemon, peeled

2 cups chamomile tea

1. Place romaine, apples, carrots, cucumber, lemon, and 1 cup of tea in a blender and blend until thoroughly combined.

2. Add remaining 1 cup of tea as needed while blending until desired consistency is achieved.

PER 1 CUP SERVING: Calories: 61 | Fat: 0g | Protein: 1g | Sodium: 26mg | Fiber: 3g | Carbohydrates: 15g

A Recipe for Sweet Dreams

Indigestion can strike at any time of day, but can be especially uncomfortable at night and can lead to painful discomfort, interrupted sleep, and moodiness. Taking a two-step approach to relieving your indigestion may help: 1) Use fruit and vegetable combinations shown to regulate stomach acid and promote more alkaline levels of the digestive tract, and 2) drink chamomile tea before bed. Chamomile tea has been shown to aid in indigestion by soothing the esophageal muscles and those of the large and small intestine.

Pineapple-Papaya Protection

Although an important ingredient, the romaine's taste is almost completely masked by the flavorful fruit combination in this recipe. This recipe not only protects the stomach lining, it is an amazing treat to be enjoyed whenever the craving for fruit strikes!

INGREDIENTS | YIELDS 3–4 CUPS

1 cup romaine lettuce

2 cups pineapple

2 cups papaya

½ lemon, peeled

¼" ginger, peeled

2 cups chamomile tea

1. Place romaine, pineapple, papaya, lemon, ginger, and 1 cup of tea in a blender and blend until thoroughly combined.

2. Add remaining 1 cup of tea as needed while blending until desired consistency is achieved.

PER 1 CUP SERVING: Calories: 69 | Fat: 0g | Protein: 1g | Sodium: 6mg | Fiber: 2g | Carbohydrates: 18g

Cucumber Cooler

*The refreshing combination of sweet citrus, crisp greens, zippy ginger,
and cooling cucumbers will perk you up while soothing your tummy. Indigestion stands no chance
against the chilling effects of this cool combo.*

INGREDIENTS | YIELDS 3–4 CUPS

1 cup watercress

1 pink grapefruit, peeled

1 orange, peeled

2 cucumbers, peeled

¼" ginger, peeled

2 cups chamomile tea

1. Place watercress, grapefruit, orange, cucumbers, ginger, and 1 cup of tea in a blender and blend until thoroughly combined.

2. Add remaining 1 cup of tea as needed while blending until desired consistency is achieved.

PER 1 CUP SERVING: Calories: 61 | Fat: 0g | Protein: 2g | Sodium: 8mg | Fiber: 3g | Carbohydrates: 14g

Ginger Ale Smoothie

*Ginger ale is the most common remedy for any type of stomach ailment.
This natural version of ginger ale provides all of the powerful nutrition
without the sometimes uncomfortable and problematic carbonation.*

INGREDIENTS | YIELDS 3–4 CUPS

1 cup watercress
4 apples, peeled and cored
¼" ginger, peeled
2 cups chamomile tea

1. Place watercress, apples, ginger, and 1 cup of tea in a blender and blend until thoroughly combined.

2. Add remaining 1 cup of tea as needed while blending until desired consistency is achieved.

PER 1 CUP SERVING: Calories: 79 | Fat: 0g | Protein: 1g | Sodium: 6mg | Fiber: 2g | Carbohydrates: 21g

Smooth Citrus for Smooth Digestion

*A delicious remedy for stomach discomfort, this banana blend
is a much sweeter and nutritious alternative to the over-the-counter antacid.*

INGREDIENTS | YIELDS 3–4 CUPS

1 cup watercress
2 cups pineapple
1 peach, pitted and peeled
1 orange, peeled
2 bananas, peeled
2 cups chamomile tea

1. Place watercress, pineapple, peach, orange, bananas, and 1 cup of tea in a blender and blend until thoroughly combined.

2. Add remaining 1 cup of tea as needed while blending until desired consistency is achieved.

PER 1 CUP SERVING: Calories: 124 | Fat: 0g | Protein: 2g | Sodium: 9mg | Fiber: 3g | Carbohydrates: 32g

Sweet Fiber

Apricots, apples, and bananas blend with sweet romaine for a delicious fiber-rich treat that will keep you clear and promote optimal digestion. Deep greens like romaine can minimize uncomfortable symptoms of indigestion.

INGREDIENTS | YIELDS 3–4 CUPS

1 cup romaine lettuce

4 apricots, peeled

2 apples, peeled and cored

1 banana, peeled

2 cups chamomile tea

1. Place romaine, apricots, apples, banana, and 1 cup of tea in a blender and blend until thoroughly combined.

2. Add remaining 1 cup of tea as needed while blending until desired consistency is achieved.

PER 1 CUP SERVING: Calories: 84 | Fat: 0g | Protein: 1g | Sodium: 4mg | Fiber: 6g | Carbohydrates: 21g

Fabulous Fiber

Fiber is absolutely necessary to promote the most efficient digestive system free of toxins, waste, and buildup that may have accrued over the years. Stock up on fiber-rich foods and blend them in delicious smoothies. Not only does blending the fiber-packed fruits and veggies make delicious meal and snack options, blending them breaks down the indigestible fiber for the best possible absorption.

Pears, Apples, and Ginger

There's not much that can compare to the sweet combination of pears, apples, and ginger. This scrumptious blend comforts your stomach with balanced nutrition in every glass.

INGREDIENTS | YIELDS 3–4 CUPS

1 cup watercress

3 apples, cored and peeled

3 pears, cored and peeled

¼" ginger, peeled

2 cups chamomile tea

1. Place watercress, apples, pears, ginger, and 1 cup of tea in a blender and blend until thoroughly combined.

2. Add remaining 1 cup of tea as needed while blending until desired consistency is achieved.

PER 1 CUP SERVING: Calories: 137 | Fat: 0g | Protein: 1g | Sodium: 7mg | Fiber: 6g | Carbohydrates: 36g

Fiber Effects of Pears

Since fiber promotes a more optimal functioning digestive tract, why not enjoy a green smoothie that packs a whopping amount of fiber from greens, pears, and apples? This delicious smoothie can get your digestive system working at its full potential and for regularity every day!

Move Over, Motion Sickness!

Cabbage is a little-known combatant for motion sickness. Blending the green leafy veggie with bananas, apples, and ginger makes a delicious remedy to this day-wrecking condition!

INGREDIENTS | YIELDS 3–4 CUPS

1 cup cabbage
3 bananas, peeled
2 apples, cored and peeled
¼" ginger, peeled
2 cups chamomile tea

1. Place cabbage, bananas, apples, ginger, and 1 cup of tea in a blender and blend until thoroughly combined.

2. Add remaining 1 cup of tea as needed while blending until desired consistency is achieved.

PER 1 CUP SERVING: Calories: 71 | Fat: 0g | Protein: 1g | Sodium: 7mg | Fiber: 2g | Carbohydrates: 18g

Heartburn, Be Gone

A tasty way to combat heartburn and provide fast-acting relief, this smoothie combines flavorful veggies that will soothe your esophagus and relieve the pain associated with acid indigestion.

INGREDIENTS | YIELDS 3–4 CUPS

1 cup spinach
2 tomatoes
3 celery stalks, leaves intact
1½ cups chamomile tea

1. Place spinach, tomatoes, celery, and ¾ cup of tea in a blender and blend until thoroughly combined.

2. Add remaining ¾ cup of tea as needed while blending until desired consistency is achieved.

PER 1 CUP SERVING: Calories: 18 | Fat: 0g | Protein: 1g | Sodium: mg | Fiber: 1g | Carbohydrates: 4g

Lifestyle Changes for Heartburn Relief

Not much can compare to the potentially disabling condition of acid reflux. Making days and nights unbearable, many people find themselves popping antacids and heartburn relievers numerous times throughout the day just to make the discomfort subside. A great way to combat this debilitating condition is to change your diet to include a wide variety of fruits and vegetables while cutting out caffeine, cigarettes, alcohol, fatty and acidic foods, and carbonation.

Spicy Stomach Soother

Spicy arugula and crisp veggies with a bite offer a deliciously savory taste combination that will soothe your stomach while calming cravings for harsh spicy foods that could aggravate digestion and lead to discomfort.

INGREDIENTS | YIELDS 3–4 CUPS

1 cup arugula

1 green onion

3 celery stalks

1 garlic clove (optional)

2 cups chamomile tea

1. Place arugula, onion, celery, garlic, and 1 cup of chamomile in a blender and blend until thoroughly combined.

2. Add remaining 1 cup of chamomile as needed while blending until desired consistency is achieved.

PER 1 CUP SERVING: Calories: 10 | Fat: 0g | Protein: 1g | Sodium: 38mg | Fiber: 1g | Carbohydrates: 2g

Get Rid of Gas!

Gas is possibly one of the most embarrassing symptoms associated with indigestion and digestive disorders. Gas-fighting foods are combined in this delicious smoothie.

INGREDIENTS | YIELDS 3–4 CUPS

1 cup spinach

2 carrots, peeled

3 celery stalks, leaves intact

¾ cup petite sweet peas

2 cups chamomile tea

1. Place spinach, carrots, celery, peas, and 1 cup of tea in a blender and blend until thoroughly combined.

2. Add remaining 1 cup of tea as needed while blending until desired consistency is achieved.

PER 1 CUP SERVING: Calories: 38 | Fat: 0g | Protein: 2g | Sodium: 80mg | Fiber: 3g | Carbohydrates: 8g

Tummy Protector

*A savory way to coat your sensitive stomach is with delicious vegetables like these.
Romaine, celery, green onion, tomatoes, and mild chamomile tea
deliver comfort and protection in every delicious sip.*

INGREDIENTS | YIELDS 3–4 CUPS

1 cup romaine lettuce

3 celery stalks, leaves intact

1 green onion

2 tomatoes

2 cups chamomile tea

1. Place romaine, celery, onion, tomatoes, and 1 cup of tea in a blender and blend until thoroughly combined.

2. Add remaining 1 cup of tea as needed while blending until desired consistency is achieved.

PER 1 CUP SERVING: Calories: 19 | Fat: 0g | Protein: 1g | Sodium: 31mg | Fiber: 2g | Carbohydrates: 4g

Red Pepper Relief

*Rich in beta-carotene, a powerful antioxidant, this veggie acts
to protect your digestive tract from dangerous cancers while also providing rich vitamins
and minerals that make for happy digestion.*

INGREDIENTS | YIELDS 3–4 CUPS

1 cup romaine lettuce

1 red bell pepper, top and seeds removed, ribs intact

2 celery stalks, leaves intact

½ lemon, peeled

1½ cups chamomile tea

1. Place romaine, red pepper, celery, lemon, and ¾ cup of tea in a blender and blend until thoroughly combined.

2. Add remaining ¾ cup of tea as needed while blending until desired consistency is achieved.

PER 1 CUP SERVING: Calories: 22 | Fat: 0g | Protein: 1g | Sodium: 27mg | Fiber: 2g | Carbohydrates: 5g

Keep It Moving

Flavorful spinach and zucchini make a splendid blend with the fresh, but lightly flavored, zucchini. Wonderfully light and delicious, this is a smoothie that will not only taste great, but relieve constipation and alleviate the uncomfortable symptoms that result!

INGREDIENTS | YIELDS 3–4 CUPS

1 cup spinach

2 zucchini, peeled

3 celery stalks, leaves intact

2 cups chamomile tea

1. Place spinach, zucchini, celery, and 1 cup of tea in a blender and blend until thoroughly combined.

2. Add remaining 1 cup of tea as needed while blending until desired consistency is achieved.

PER 1 CUP SERVING: Calories: 22 | Fat: 0g | Protein: 2g | Sodium: 42mg | Fiber: 2g | Carbohydrates: 5g

Produce for Constipation Relief

Constipation can really slow you down! The irritating condition can make you feel lethargic, uncomfortable, and irritable. Stay regular by including the recommended 5 servings of fruits and veggies daily. All of this produce contains lots of fiber, which relieves constipation.

Cabbage Calms Indigestion

This delightful combination of cabbage and cruciferous veggies packs a punch in providing rich vitamins and minerals. It aids in digestion with its rich sources of vitamin K and carotenes that combine to act as an anti-inflammatory.

INGREDIENTS | YIELDS 3–4 CUPS

1 cup cabbage

1 cup broccoli

1 cup cauliflower

1 garlic clove (optional)

2 cups chamomile tea

1. Place cabbage, broccoli, cauliflower, garlic, and 1 cup of tea in a blender and blend until thoroughly combined.

2. Add remaining 1 cup of tea as needed while blending until desired consistency is achieved.

PER 1 CUP SERVING: Calories: 20 | Fat: 0g | Protein: 1g | Sodium: 21mg | Fiber: 2g | Carbohydrates: 4g

Mega Magnesium

With powerful stores of minerals, especially magnesium, the veggies in this recipe promote easier digestion along with overall health for your entire body and mind.

INGREDIENTS | YIELDS 3–4 CUPS

1 cup cabbage

1 cup broccoli

1 cup cauliflower

2 celery stalks, leaves intact

2 cups chamomile tea

1. Place cabbage, broccoli, cauliflower, celery, and 1 cup of tea in a blender and blend until thoroughly combined.

2. Add remaining 1 cup of tea as needed while blending until desired consistency is achieved.

PER 1 CUP SERVING: Calories: 23 | Fat: 0g | Protein: 2g | Sodium: 37mg | Fiber: 2g | Carbohydrates: 5g

Magnesium Benefits

This powerful mineral is responsible for the proper functioning of our muscles and nerves, so it is very important to men and women at any age and any lifestyle. Deficiencies in magnesium can lead to debilitating conditions like diabetes, hypertension, osteoporosis, and irritable bowel syndrome. It can also negatively affect digestion by reducing its natural calming effect on muscle spasms and impairing the strength of the muscles associated with digestion.

The Constipation Cure

Cure the most uncomfortable indigestion symptoms like constipation with delicious smoothies like this one, which features a delicious blend of sweet and crisp vegetables.

INGREDIENTS | YIELDS 3–4 CUPS

1 cup romaine

1 cup asparagus

1 cup broccoli

2 carrots, peeled

2 cups chamomile tea

1. Place romaine, asparagus, broccoli, carrots, and 1 cup of tea in a blender and blend until thoroughly combined.

2. Add remaining 1 cup of tea as needed while blending until desired consistency is achieved.

PER 1 CUP SERVING: Calories: 29 | Fat: 0g | Protein: 1g | Sodium: 33mg | Fiber: 2g | Carbohydrates: 6g

Cool Off Colitis

Remedy this terrible digestive disorder with vegetables rich in vitamin E! Spinach, asparagus, carrots, tomato, and light chamomile make for a savory, yet slightly sweet, smoothie.

INGREDIENTS | YIELDS 3–4 CUPS

1 cup spinach

1 cup asparagus

3 carrots, peeled

1 tomato

2 cups chamomile tea

1. Place spinach, asparagus, carrots, tomato, and 1 cup of tea in a blender and blend until thoroughly combined.

2. Add remaining 1 cup of tea as needed while blending until desired consistency is achieved.

PER 1 CUP SERVING: Calories: 33 | Fat: 0g | Protein: 2g | Sodium: 42mg | Fiber: 3g | Carbohydrates: 7g

CHAPTER 16

Fantastic Kid-Friendly Smoothies

Cantaloupe Quencher

Kids love fresh cantaloupe! Juice running down their little chins, they can't get enough of this powerful vitamin-rich fruit, which makes it the perfect star of a green smoothie recipe like this one.

INGREDIENTS | YIELDS 3–4 CUPS

1 cup iceberg lettuce

2 cups cantaloupe, rind and seeds removed

2 bananas, peeled

1 cup almond milk

1 cup ice

Protect Your Family with Vitamins and Antioxidants

Although many people get the flu shot, exercise regularly, and try to eat a diet that will promote illness protection, when was the last time your child was guzzling vitamin C for the health benefits or finishing off his spinach because of the rich iron content? Children eat what tastes great, and when you make nutritious food delicious, they arm their own bodies with immunity-building protection.

1. Place iceberg, cantaloupe, bananas, and ½ cup almond milk in a blender and blend until thoroughly combined.

2. Add remaining ½ cup almond milk and ice as needed while blending until desired consistency is achieved.

PER 1 CUP SERVING: Calories: 91 | Fat: 1g | Protein: 1g | Sodium: 47mg | Fiber: 2g | Carbohydrates: 21g

Wonder Watermelon

Watermelon's super powers don't end with its amazing hydrating effects, which make it one of the top go-to summer fruits. This delicious smoothie with the hidden taste of romaine will make a veggie eater of your pickiest eater!

INGREDIENTS | YIELDS 3–4 CUPS

1 cup romaine lettuce

2 cups watermelon, rind and seeds removed

2 bananas, peeled

½ cup Greek-style yogurt

1 cup ice

1. Place romaine, watermelon, bananas, and yogurt in a blender and blend until thoroughly combined.

2. Add ice as needed while blending until desired consistency is achieved.

PER 1 CUP SERVING: Calories: 82 | Fat: 0g | Protein: 4g | Sodium: 15mg | Fiber: 2g | Carbohydrates: 18g

A Great Gatorade Alternative

Packed with delicious flavor and hydrating power, watermelon offers up the added benefit of much-needed electrolytes for active kids. Most commercial drinks that promise a boost of balancing electrolytes are packed with sugars and not nutrition! Sweet homemade green smoothies are a smarter choice for your youngster following any high-endurance activity.

Honeydew for Your Honeys

*This smooth, slightly sweet treat is delicious without being overpowering.
With a very cool color and a taste your kids will love, this recipe makes a fruity green milkshake
that delivers loads of vitamins and minerals and only tastes like a sinful treat!*

INGREDIENTS | YIELDS 3–4 CUPS

1 cup romaine lettuce

2 cups honeydew, rind and seeds removed

2 bananas, peeled

½ cup Greek-style yogurt

1 cup ice

1. Place romaine, honeydew, bananas, and yogurt in a blender and blend until thoroughly combined.

2. Add ice as needed while blending until desired consistency is achieved.

PER 1 CUP SERVING: Calories: 101 | Fat: 0g | Protein: 4g | Sodium: 29mg | Fiber: 2g | Carbohydrates: 23g

Strawberry Breakfast Smoothie

*A deliciously rich strawberry banana smoothie will be your
kids' favorite breakfast after just one taste.*

INGREDIENTS | YIELDS 3–4 CUPS

1 cup romaine lettuce

2 pints strawberries

2 bananas, peeled

1 cup strawberry kefir

1 cup ice

1. Place romaine, strawberries, bananas, and kefir in a blender and blend until thoroughly combined.

2. Add ice as needed while blending until desired consistency is achieved.

PER 1 CUP SERVING: Calories: 136 | Fat: 1g | Protein: 5g | Sodium: 35mg | Fiber: 5g | Carbohydrates: 30g

Blueberry Burst

Even kids who say they hate blueberries love this smoothie.
Tasting more like ice cream than a green smoothie, this blueberry treat
is chock full of vitamins and minerals with a taste your kids will crave.

INGREDIENTS | YIELDS 3–4 CUPS

1 cup watercress

2 pints blueberries

2 bananas, peeled

1 cup blueberry kefir

1 cup ice

Blueberries and Bananas for Overall Health

Not only does the delicious blend of blueberries and bananas taste great, this combination makes an amazingly nutritional treat for youngsters. The rich potassium, magnesium, B6, and electrolyte stores of the bananas add to the vitamin C, sapronins, and powerful antioxidants of the blueberries. It's a delicious way to promote heart health, mental clarity and focus, energy, and immune-fighting power!

1. Place watercress, blueberries, bananas, and kefir in a blender container and blend until thoroughly combined.

2. Add ice as needed while blending until desired consistency is achieved.

PER 1 CUP SERVING: Calories: 173 | Fat: 1g | Protein: 5g | Sodium: 38mg | Fiber: 5g | Carbohydrates: 40g

Green Machine

This smoothie appeals to youngsters because the overall taste
is sweet and the color is very different from ordinary juices.
This flavorful combination is a nutrition-packed drink for any child or adult.

INGREDIENTS | YIELDS 3–4 CUPS

1 cup spinach

4 Granny Smith apples, peeled and cored

2 bananas, peeled

2 cups purified water

1 cup ice

1. Place spinach, apples, bananas, and 1 cup of water in a blender and blend until thoroughly combined.

2. Add remaining 1 cup of water and ice as needed while blending until desired consistency is achieved.

PER 1 CUP SERVING: Calories: 132 | Fat: 0g | Protein: 1g | Sodium: 10mg | Fiber: 4g | Carbohydrates: 34g

Lead By Example

Monkey see, monkey do. Kids look up to their parents for cues on what is desirable in dealing with everything from speech to behavior to food likes and dislikes. Show your child that you indulge in green smoothies and enjoy them; you'll be nurturing yourself with powerful nutrition while being a positive role model. You'll discourage your child from being a picky eater, and she'll reap the benefits of a healthy, balanced diet.

Sweet Pumpkin Pie

Masking an entire cup of spinach in the delicious flavors of sweet pie is an excellent idea! Sweet potatoes and almond milk, along with intense aromatic spices, will never give away the star ingredient: spinach!

INGREDIENTS | YIELDS 3–4 CUPS

1 cup spinach

2 sweet potatoes, peeled

1 teaspoon cinnamon

1 teaspoon pumpkin pie spice

2 cups almond milk

1 cup ice

1. Place spinach, sweet potatoes, cinnamon, pumpkin pie spice, and 1 cup almond milk in a blender and blend until thoroughly combined.

2. Add remaining 1 cup of almond milk and ice as needed while blending until desired consistency is achieved.

PER 1 CUP SERVING: Calories: 134 | Fat: 1g | Protein: 2g | Sodium: 88mg | Fiber: 3g | Carbohydrates: 29g

Green Lemonade

Delicious on any hot day, most kids won't pass up lemonade!
Revamp the old nutrition-lacking version of lemonade by blending this delicious mix of real lemons,
sweet apples, raw honey or agave nectar, vitamin-rich spinach, and green tea.

INGREDIENTS | YIELDS 3–4 CUPS

1 cup spinach

2 apples, peeled and cored

4 lemons, peeled

1 tablespoon raw honey or agave nectar

2 cups green tea

1 cup ice

1. Place spinach, apples, lemons, honey or agave, and 1 cup of tea in a blender and blend until thoroughly combined.

2. Add remaining 1 cup of tea and ice as needed while blending until desired consistency is achieved.

PER 1 CUP SERVING: Calories: 74 | Fat: 0g | Protein: 1g | Sodium: 7mg | Fiber: 3g | Carbohydrates: 21g

Grapefruit Tangerine

Grapefruit can pack a punch with tart taste, but combining it with tangerines, pineapple, and soothing green tea makes a delicious balance of flavors for one remarkably sweet and refreshing smoothie your kids will enjoy.

INGREDIENTS | YIELDS 3–4 CUPS

1 cup watercress
2 grapefruits, peeled
2 tangerines, peeled
1 cup pineapple
1 cup green tea
1 cup ice

1. Place watercress, grapefruits, tangerines, pineapple, and ½ cup tea in a blender and blend until thoroughly combined.

2. Add remaining ½ cup tea and ice as needed while blending until desired consistency is achieved.

PER 1 CUP SERVING: Calories: 63 | Fat: 0g | Protein: 1g | Sodium: 6mg | Fiber: 1g | Carbohydrates: 16g

Chocolate Banana Blitz

Kids love chocolate! A brilliant way to transform a plain old green vegetable into pure deliciousness for a child is to add chocolatey carob for a taste sensation that will create your kids' favorite fake-out of all!

INGREDIENTS | YIELDS 3–4 CUPS

1 cup romaine lettuce
2 tablespoons carob powder
3 bananas, peeled
Pulp of 1 vanilla bean or 1 teaspoon vanilla extract
1 cup vanilla kefir
1 cup ice

1. Place romaine, carob powder, bananas, vanilla, and kefir in a blender and blend until thoroughly combined.

2. Add ice as needed while blending until desired consistency is achieved.

PER 1 CUP SERVING: Calories: 122 | Fat: 1g | Protein: 4g | Sodium: 35mg | Fiber: 3g | Carbohydrates: 26g

The Chocolate Alternatives

Powdered raw cacao and carob are two alternatives to the not-so-healthy chocolate enhanced with sugars that can bring out undesirable overstimulation in your little one. By including the flavors of the chocolate alternatives, you can provide a chocolate-flavored delight packed with rich antioxidants and amazing vitamins and minerals. Healthy, no sugar, no additives, no guilt!

Great Grape

With balanced nutrition and a great taste your kids will love,
this is one sweet treat you'll never feel guilty about giving them!

INGREDIENTS | YIELDS 3–4 CUPS

1 cup watercress

3 cups grapes

2 pears, cored and peeled

1 cup almond milk

1 cup ice

1. Place watercress, grapes, pears, and almond milk in a blender and blend until thoroughly combined.

2. Add ice as needed while blending until desired consistency is achieved.

PER 1 CUP SERVING: Calories: 153 | Fat: 1g | Protein: 2g | Sodium: 45mg | Fiber: 4g | Carbohydrates: 38g

Peas, Please!

This veggie-packed smoothie actually tastes sweet! If your kiddies like peas and love carrots, this smoothie's a sure thing; if your kiddo is antiveggie, this smoothie's probably going to get him to admit they're not half bad.

INGREDIENTS | YIELDS 3–4 CUPS

1 cup spinach

1 cup sweet peas

2 carrots, peeled

1 apple, peeled and cored

1 cup green tea

1 cup ice

1. Place spinach, peas, carrots, apple, and tea in a blender and blend until thoroughly combined.

2. Add ice as needed while blending until desired consistency is achieved.

PER 1 CUP SERVING: Calories: 60 | Fat: 0g | Protein: 2g | Sodium: 64mg | Fiber: 3g | Carbohydrates: 13g

The Lonely Sweet Pea

Very rarely do kids get heaping helpings of peas on a regular basis. Providing more than 50 percent of the recommended daily amount of vitamin K and packed with vitamin Bs and C, folate, iron, zinc, manganese, and protein, peas are a great choice for any child's diet. Promoting brain health, bone strength, heart health, and disease-fighting protection, these sweet green morsels are worth their weight in health!

Citrus Burst

*For kids who love citrus fruits, this recipe is absolutely amazing.
Blending an entire cup of greens into a deliciously sweet, tangy, and delightfully
refreshing treat for any age, this is one great-tasting way to get fiber.*

INGREDIENTS | YIELDS 3–4 CUPS

1 cup watercress

3 cups pineapple

1 tangerine, peeled

½ lemon, peeled

1 cup Greek-style yogurt

1 cup ice

1. Place watercress, pineapple, tangerine, lemon, and yogurt in a blender and blend until thoroughly combined.

2. Add ice as needed while blending until desired consistency is achieved.

PER 1 CUP SERVING: Calories: 103 | Fat: 0g | Protein: 7g | Sodium: 30mg | Fiber: 1g | Carbohydrates: 21g

Peaches 'n Cream

Fresh or frozen ingredients, fireside or poolside, this smoothie is a mouthwatering way to deliver fresh ingredients, no added sugars, an entire cup of greens, and plentiful fruit servings to kids who need and deserve great-tasting nutrition.

INGREDIENTS | YIELDS 3–4 CUPS

1 cup romaine lettuce
3 peaches, pitted
2 bananas, peeled
1 cup vanilla kefir
1 cup ice

1. Place romaine, peaches, bananas, and kefir in a blender and blend until thoroughly combined.

2. Add ice as needed while blending until desired consistency is achieved.

PER 1 CUP SERVING: Calories: 133 | Fat: 1g | Protein: 5g | Sodium: 34mg | Fiber: 3g | Carbohydrates: 30g

Sweet Pears

Pears have a unique flavor that blends deliciously with the crisp watercress, sweet bananas, and outrageously delicious kefir to make an amazing blend of fruits and vegetables. It provides intense vitamins and minerals in every scrumptious sip!

INGREDIENTS | YIELDS 3–4 CUPS

1 cup watercress

4 pears, peeled and cored

2 bananas, peeled

2 cups vanilla kefir

1 cup ice

1. Place watercress, pears, bananas, and 1 cup of kefir in a blender and blend until thoroughly combined.

2. Add remaining 1 cup of kefir and ice as needed while blending until desired consistency is achieved.

PER 1 CUP SERVING: Calories: 192 | Fat: 1g | Protein: 4g | Sodium: 38mg | Fiber: 7g | Carbohydrates: 46g

Vanilla Banana Bonkers

At least if your child does go bonkers, you'll know it's from the rich vitamin, mineral, antioxidant, and probiotic power of these amazing ingredients.

INGREDIENTS | YIELDS 3–4 CUPS

1 cup romaine lettuce

4 bananas, peeled

Pulp of 1½ vanilla beans or 1½ teaspoons vanilla extract

2 cups vanilla kefir

1 cup ice

1. Place romaine, bananas, vanilla, and 1 cup kefir in a blender and blend until thoroughly combined.

2. Add remaining 1 cup of kefir and ice as needed while blending until desired consistency is achieved.

PER 1 CUP SERVING: Calories: 98 | Fat: 1g | Protein: 6g | Sodium: 65mg | Fiber: 1g | Carbohydrates: 17g

Cherry Vanilla Milkshake

This recipe is one for the serious doubters who don't believe a child will consume greens blended in a smoothie. Vitamin-rich spinach, vibrant cherries, sweet banana, and vanilla bean combine with creamy kefir for a cherry vanilla milkshake!

INGREDIENTS | YIELDS 3–4 CUPS

1 cup spinach

2 cups cherries, pitted

1 banana, peeled

Pulp of 1½ vanilla beans or 1½ teaspoons vanilla extract

2 cups vanilla kefir

1 cup ice

1. Place spinach, cherries, banana, vanilla, and 1 cup of kefir in a blender and blend until thoroughly combined.

2. Add remaining 1 cup of kefir and ice as needed while blending until desired consistency is achieved.

PER 1 CUP SERVING: Calories: 146 | Fat: 0g | Protein: 7g | Sodium: 70mg | Fiber: 3g | Carbohydrates: 29g

Chocolate Dream

Your little ones and their sometimes more stubborn elders will fall for the deliciously rich flavors of this recipe, with the only question being, "Are there seconds?"

INGREDIENTS | YIELDS 3–4 CUPS

1 cup spinach

2 tablespoons carob powder

3 bananas, peeled

2 cups almond milk

1 cup ice

1. Place spinach, carob, bananas, and 1 cup almond milk in a blender and blend until thoroughly combined.

2. Add remaining 1 cup of almond milk and ice as needed while blending until desired consistency is achieved.

PER 1 CUP SERVING: Calories: 153 | Fat: 2g | Protein: 2g | Sodium: 84mg | Fiber: 4g | Carbohydrates: 35g

Nuts 'n Honey

Trail mixes, cereals, granola, and even candy bars make this delicious and healthy blend of ingredients a sugar-packed, preservative-enhanced trap! Combining these fresh ingredients at home, you'll know exactly where the ingredients came from.

INGREDIENTS | YIELDS 3–4 CUPS

⅛ cup almonds

⅛ cup walnuts

1 tablespoon ground flaxseeds

2 cups almond milk

1 cup romaine lettuce

2 bananas, peeled

1½ tablespoons raw honey or agave nectar

1 cup ice

1. Combine nuts, flax, and 1 cup almond milk in a blender and emulsify until no nut bits remain.

2. Add romaine, bananas, and agave or honey and blend until thoroughly combined.

3. Add remaining 1 cup of almond milk and ice as needed while blending until desired consistency is achieved.

PER 1 CUP SERVING: Calories: 173 | Fat: 7g | Protein: 3g | Sodium: 78mg | Fiber: 4g | Carbohydrates: 28g

Flaxseeds for Kids

If your child isn't wild about salmon, or any fish for that matter, you can add omega-3s to his diet in an undetectable form. Ground flaxseeds provide a mild nutty flavor without an extreme taste. Sold at grocery stores and mega marts around the country, organic ground flaxseeds are an inexpensive way to boost your child's omegas.

Pineapple Melon

Sweet pineapple and the naturally syrupy cantaloupe make a delicious duo in this amazing recipe. Your kids will only recognize the flavors of the sweet citrus and melon.

INGREDIENTS | YIELDS 3–4 CUPS

1 cup romaine lettuce

2 cups pineapple

2 cups cantaloupe, rind and seeds removed

1 cup green tea

1 cup ice

1. Place romaine, pineapple, cantaloupe, and ½ cup tea in a blender and blend until thoroughly combined.

2. Add remaining ½ cup of tea and ice as needed while blending until desired consistency is achieved.

PER 1 CUP SERVING: Calories: 66 | Fat: 0g | Protein: 1g | Sodium: 15mg | Fiber: 1g | Carbohydrates: 17g

Very Vitamin C!

Big helpings of vitamin C–rich fruits, mineral-boasting greens, and delicious chamomile combine for an amazingly refreshing and sweet breakfast, lunch, snack, or dessert.

INGREDIENTS | YIELDS 3–4 CUPS

1 cup watercress

2 tangerines, peeled

2 cups pineapple

1 cup grapefruit

1 cup green tea

1 cup ice

1. Place watercress, tangerines, pineapple, grapefruit, and ½ cup tea in a blender and blend until thoroughly combined.

2. Add remaining ½ cup tea and ice as needed while blending until desired consistency is achieved.

PER 1 CUP SERVING: Calories: 100 | Fat: 0g | Protein: 2g | Sodium: 5mg | Fiber: 2g | Carbohydrates: 26g

CHAPTER 17

Smoothies for Pets

Dog's Desire

Dogs love green beans and carrots! This tasty combination provides intense vitamins and minerals. Blend until thick but combined, and serve alone or with dry food.

INGREDIENTS | YIELDS 3–4 CUPS

1 cup romaine lettuce

2 cups green beans

2 carrots, greens removed

2 cups purified water

Cats and Veggies

Because of the very different digestive system of cats, recipes that include excessive greens and vegetables are not recommended. While dogs are able to better digest greens and starchy veggies, cats have great difficulty digesting cellulose (plant fibers) and can suffer vomiting or diarrhea as a result of consuming too much. Take care of your kitty by limiting the plant composition of his smoothie to 1 cup of greens per recipe.

1. Place romaine, green beans, carrots, and water in a blender and blend until thoroughly combined and thick consistency is achieved.

2. Serve alone or combined with dry food.

PER 1 CUP SERVING: Calories: 32 | Fat: 0g | Protein: 1g | Sodium: 28mg | Fiber: 3g | Carbohydrates: 7g

Some Extra Wag in That Tail

Wheatgrass and green beans combine for a delicious treat your dog is sure to love! Providing vitamins and minerals that promote health in a tasty combination, you can be sure your dog is getting just what he wants and deserves.

INGREDIENTS | YIELDS 3–4 CUPS

1 cup wheatgrass
2 cups green beans
2 cups purified water

1. Place wheatgrass, green beans, and water in a blender and blend until thoroughly combined.

2. Serve alone or combined with dry food.

PER 1 CUP SERVING: Calories: 31 | Fat: 0g | Protein: 1g | Sodium: 16mg | Fiber: 2g | Carbohydrates: 6g

Fruit for Man's Best Friend

Cantaloupe and honeydew mix with spinach to make a sweet blend that's a delightful difference from the same old kibble. Providing antioxidants for health and immunity-building protection, this combo is a tasty way to deliver important nutrition to your best buddy.

INGREDIENTS | YIELDS 3–4 CUPS

1 cup spinach

1 cup cantaloupe, rind and seeds removed

1 cup honeydew, rind and seeds removed

2 cups purified water

1. Place spinach, cantaloupe, honeydew, and water in a blender and blend until thoroughly combined.

2. Serve alone or combined with dry food.

PER 1 CUP SERVING: Calories: 30 | Fat: 0g | Protein: 1g | Sodium: 22mg | Fiber: 1g | Carbohydrates: 8g

A Coat to Envy

Cucumbers aren't just for humans. Packed with high water content and amazing nutrition, this delightful blend of cucumbers, romaine, and mangoes has vitamins and minerals in a great-tasting dish for your furry friend, who will shine!

INGREDIENTS | YIELDS 3–4 CUPS

1 cup romaine lettuce

1 cup cucumber

1 cup mango

2 cups purified water

1. Place romaine, cucumber, mango, and water in a blender and blend until thoroughly combined.

2. Serve alone or combined with dry food.

PER 1 CUP SERVING: Calories: 33 | Fat: 0g | Protein: 1g | Sodium: 5mg | Fiber: 1g | Carbohydrates: 8g

Hair That Shines

The same vitamins and minerals that make human hair radiant can also work wonders on your dog's coat! Improve the health and shine of your dog's hair by including silica-containing vegetables like cucumbers. The biotin of the green leafy vegetables used in green smoothies also promotes natural health and strength for your dog's hair and nails.

Whiter Teeth for Rover

*Strawberries have amazing whitening effects in the human mouth,
and the same whitening power can also work wonders for your pup. Serve this delightful smoothie
for whiter teeth, better breath, and health benefits galore!*

INGREDIENTS | YIELDS 3–4 CUPS

1 cup radicchio
1 cup strawberries, hulls removed
1 banana, peeled
2 cups purified water

1. Place radicchio, strawberries, banana, and water in a blender and blend until thoroughly combined.

2. Serve alone or combined with dry food.

PER 1 CUP SERVING: Calories: 40 | Fat: 0g | Protein: 1g | Sodium: 5mg | Fiber: 2g | Carbohydrates: 10g

Extra Energy for Playtime

*Complex carbohydrates and important protein combine for amazing sustainable energy
that will make playtime more enjoyable for everyone.*

INGREDIENTS | YIELDS 3–4 CUPS

1 cup romaine lettuce
2 cup green beans
1 cup raw chicken breast
2 cups purified water

1. Place romaine, green beans, chicken, and water in a blender and blend until thoroughly combined.

2. Serve alone or combined with dry food.

PER 1 CUP SERVING: Calories: 50 | Fat: 0g | Protein: 8g | Sodium: 25mg | Fiber: 2g | Carbohydrates: 4g

Raw Food Warning

There is a movement of people who feed their pets a natural or raw diet (the Biologically Appropriate Raw Food or BARF diet). However, there appears to be a risk of bacterial infection, e.g., salmonella, to the pet as well as a risk of parasitic infection. There is also the risk of human exposure to these pathogens through the pet's stool. Extra care must be taken to minimize the risk, both during food preparation and stool removal.

The Cat's Meow

Rich meat and a light veggie flavor combine for a delicious and nutritious meal or snack for your favorite feline friend. Picky eaters rejoice for the delicious flavors of chicken and light vegetables!

INGREDIENTS | YIELDS 3–4 CUPS

1 cup romaine lettuce

1 cup raw chicken breast

1 sardine

2 cups purified water

Friendly Meals for Felines and Canines

Kitties aren't the only fans of fish. As natural hunters, dogs are just as welcoming as cats when it comes to including fish in any meal. Providing protein, omega-3 fatty acids, and an abundance of vitamins and minerals, dogs equally enjoy this delightful fish and light veggie blend.

1. Place romaine, chicken, sardine, and water in a blender and blend until thoroughly combined.

2. Serve alone or combined with dry food.

PER 1 CUP SERVING: Calories: 39 | Fat: 1g | Protein: 7g | Sodium: 37mg | Fiber: 0g | Carbohydrates: 0g

A Fishy Favorite

Cats are notorious for loving fish of all kinds . . . dead or alive!
Fulfill their need for omega-3s with this delicious recipe of salmon and light greens.

INGREDIENTS | YIELDS 3–4 CUPS

1 cup romaine lettuce

1 cup raw salmon, with bones

2 cups purified water

Taurine for Cats

From promoting everything from reproductive health and eye health to the prevention of heart disease, taurine is an essential amino acid needed by cats. Not required for proper functioning of dogs, taurine is an important element of a cat's diet that can only be acquired from animal products like meats, fish, and eggs.

1. Place romaine, salmon, and water in a blender and blend until thoroughly combined.

2. Serve alone or combined with dry food.

PER 1 CUP SERVING: Calories: 34 | Fat: 1g | Protein: 6g | Sodium: 22mg | Fiber: 0g | Carbohydrates: 0g

A Meaty Medley

Packed with raw meats and delicious veggies,
this is sure to be one of your dog's most exciting meals!

INGREDIENTS | YIELDS 3–4 CUPS

1 cup romaine lettuce

1 cup raw beef steak pieces

1 cup green beans

2 carrots, greens removed

2 cups purified water

1. Place romaine, beef, green beans, carrots, and water in a blender and blend until thoroughly combined.

2. Serve alone or combined with dry food.

PER 1 CUP SERVING: Calories: 92 | Fat: 6g | Protein: 6g | Sodium: 45mg | Fiber: 2g | Carbohydrates: 5g

No Bones about It

Although dogs love the leftover bones from your meaty meal, the bones that are usually enjoyed are large enough that choking is not a possibility. These should be served on the side of these blended recipes as opposed to being included. Taking care to remove the bones from meats in your blended meals will ensure that your furry friend is safe from harm and doesn't experience vomiting from indigestible bone fragments.

Salmon Sardine Blend

Because cats and dogs are both fans of their swimming friends, this recipe can be catered to either pet. For cats, blend the fish with bones included; for dogs, blend fish without.

INGREDIENTS | YIELDS 3–4 CUPS

1 cup iceberg lettuce

½ cup salmon (bones included for cats)

½ cup sardines (bones included for cats)

½ cup fresh fish of choice (bones included for cats)

2 cups purified water

1. Place iceberg, salmon, sardines, choice fish, and water in a blender and blend until thoroughly combined.

2. Serve alone or combined with dry food.

PER 1 CUP SERVING: Calories: 69 | Fat: 3g | Protein: 10g | Sodium: 115mg | Fiber: 0g | Carbohydrates: 1g

Bones in Cat Food?

When cats consume whole animals caught in a hunt, they use the bones for cleansing purposes. Although they can be chewed and digested, the main benefit of including bones in cat food is to clean the cat's teeth. Being careful enough to make bones noticeably large enough to remove or small enough to prevent choking, you can ensure your cat's safety by ensuring the bones are of suitable size before adding them to the fishy feast.

A Fruity Favorite

Pineapple, blueberry, and banana sounds delicious enough for a breakfast blend to get your day going; this recipe, though, is for your four-legged friend!

INGREDIENTS | YIELDS 3–4 CUPS

1 cup watercress

½ cup pineapple

1 cup blueberries

1 banana, peeled

2 cups purified water

Cater to Your Dog's Likes and Dislikes

Because dogs are lovers of some fruits but not all, manipulate ingredients within the green smoothies to coincide with your pet's flavor preferences. Most fruits can be substituted for something similar in weight and water concentration in order to allow the other ingredients' amounts to remain the same.

1. Place watercress, pineapple, blueberries, banana, and water in a blender and blend until thoroughly combined.

2. Serve alone or combine with dry food.

PER 1 CUP SERVING: Calories: 58 | Fat: 0g | Protein: 1g | Sodium: 7mg | Fiber: 2g | Carbohydrates: 15g

Chicken Without the Chase

Suitable for dogs only because of the peas and corn, this tasty combination of white meat and veggies will be a delightful treat packed with protein, vitamins, and minerals for your yapping loved one.

INGREDIENTS | YIELDS 3–4 CUPS

1 cup romaine lettuce
1 cup raw chicken breast
½ cup peas
½ cup corn
2 cups water

1. Place romaine, chicken, peas, corn, and water in a blender and blend until thoroughly combined.

2. Serve alone or combined with dry food.

PER 1 CUP SERVING: Calories: 62 | Fat: 1g | Protein: 8g | Sodium: 42mg | Fiber: 2g | Carbohydrates: 6g

Yummy Lamb

Lamb can make a splendid treat for both dogs and cats. Raw meat pieces without the bones are recommended for blends for dogs; bones are suggested for blends catered to cats.

INGREDIENTS | YIELDS 3–4 CUPS

1 cup romaine lettuce
1 cup lamb pieces, deboned
1½ cups purified water

1. Place romaine, lamb, and water in a blender and blend until thoroughly combined.

2. Serve alone or combined with dry food.

PER 1 CUP SERVING: Calories: 72 | Fat: 4g | Protein: 7g | Sodium: 25mg | Fiber: 0g | Carbohydrates: 1g

Salmon Surprise

Salmon is delicious, so imagine how fragrant it is to your four-legged friends! No need for a dinner bell with this recipe.

INGREDIENTS | YIELDS 3–4 CUPS

1 cup romaine lettuce

2 cups salmon (bones included for cats)

2 cups purified water

Omega-3s for Pets

Although some pet foods are fortified with omega-3s, fresh fish is best when delivering this nutrient to your pet. Because both cats and dogs are fans of fish, the meal can be a tasty way of providing a meal rich in omega-3s without turning to additives or fortified foods.

1. Place romaine, salmon, and water in a blender and blend until thoroughly combined.

2. Serve alone or combined with dry foods.

PER 1 CUP SERVING: Calories: 67 | Fat: 2g | Protein: 11g | Sodium: 41mg | Fiber: 0g | Carbohydrates: 0g

Standard U.S./Metric Measurement Conversions

VOLUME CONVERSIONS

U.S. Volume Measure	Metric Equivalent
⅛ teaspoon	0.5 milliliters
¼ teaspoon	1 milliliters
½ teaspoon	2 milliliters
1 teaspoon	5 milliliters
½ tablespoon	7 milliliters
1 tablespoon (3 teaspoons)	15 milliliters
2 tablespoons (1 fluid ounce)	30 milliliters
¼ cup (4 tablespoons)	60 milliliters
⅓ cup	90 milliliters
½ cup (4 fluid ounces)	125 milliliters
⅔ cup	160 milliliters
¾ cup (6 fluid ounces)	180 milliliters
1 cup (16 tablespoons)	250 milliliters
1 pint (2 cups)	500 milliliters
1 quart (4 cups)	1 liter (about)

WEIGHT CONVERSIONS

U.S. Weight Measure	Metric Equivalent
½ ounce	15 grams
1 ounce	30 grams
2 ounces	60 grams
3 ounces	85 grams
¼ pound (4 ounces)	115 grams
½ pound (8 ounces)	225 grams
¾ pound (12 ounces)	340 grams
1 pound (16 ounces)	454 grams

OVEN TEMPERATURE CONVERSIONS

Degrees Fahrenheit	Degrees Celsius
200 degrees F	100 degrees C
250 degrees F	120 degrees C
275 degrees F	140 degrees C
300 degrees F	150 degrees C
325 degrees F	160 degrees C
350 degrees F	180 degrees C
375 degrees F	190 degrees C
400 degrees F	200 degrees C
425 degrees F	220 degrees C
450 degrees F	230 degrees C

BAKING PAN SIZES

American	Metric
8 × 1½ inch round baking pan	20 × 4 cm cake tin
9 × 1½ inch round baking pan	23 × 3.5 cm cake tin
1 × 7 × 1½ inch baking pan	28 × 18 × 4 cm baking tin
13 × 9 × 2 inch baking pan	30 × 20 × 5 cm baking tin
2 quart rectangular baking dish	30 × 20 × 3 cm baking tin
15 × 10 × 2 inch baking pan	30 × 25 × 2 cm baking tin (Swiss roll tin)
9 inch pie plate	22 × 4 or 23 × 4 cm pie plate
7 or 8 inch springform pan	18 or 20 cm springform or loose bottom cake tin
9 × 5 × 3 inch loaf pan	23 × 13 × 7 cm or 2 lb narrow loaf or pate tin
1½ quart casserole	1.5 liter casserole
2 quart casserole	2 liter casserole

Index

We Have
EVERYTHING
on Anything!

With more than 19 million copies sold, the Everything® series has become one of America's favorite resources for solving problems, learning new skills, and organizing lives. Our brand is not only recognizable—it's also welcomed.

The series is a hand-in-hand partner for people who are ready to tackle new subjects—like you!

For more information on the Everything® series, please visit *www.adamsmedia.com*

The Everything® list spans a wide range of subjects, with more than 500 titles covering 25 different categories:

Business	History	Reference
Careers	Home Improvement	Religion
Children's Storybooks	Everything Kids	Self-Help
Computers	Languages	Sports & Fitness
Cooking	Music	Travel
Crafts and Hobbies	New Age	Wedding
Education/Schools	Parenting	Writing
Games and Puzzles	Personal Finance	
Health	Pets	